EXPLORING ENVIRONMENTS

Authors
Sheryl Mercier and Evalyn Hoover

Editors
Evalyn Hoover and Betty Cordel

Illustrator
Sheryl Mercier

Desktop Publisher
Kristy Shuler-Russell

Contributors
Brenda Richmond and David Mitchell

Content Consultant
Dr. Ben Van Wagner

This book contains materials developed by the AIMS Education Foundation. **AIMS** (**A**ctivities **I**ntegrating **M**athematics and **S**cience) began in 1981 with a grant from the National Science Foundation. The non-profit AIMS Education Foundation publishes hands-on instructional materials (books and the monthly magazine) that integrate curricular disciplines such as mathematics, science, language arts, and social studies. The Foundation sponsors a national program of professional development through which educators may gain both an understanding of the AIMS philosophy and expertise in teaching by integrated, hands-on methods.

ISBN **1-881431-77-0**

Printed in the United States of America

TABLE OF CONTENTS

National Standards Alignment 1
Purpose 4
Sample Science Careers 5
Materials and Management Suggestions 6

Grades K–2
Plans and Activities 8
Developing Ideas 9
Application of Knowledge 10
Curriculum Correlation 12

Grades 3–4
Plans and Activities 14
Developing Ideas 15
Application of Knowledge 16
Curriculum Correlation 19

Grades 5–6
Plans and Activities 21
Developing Ideas 22
Application of Knowledge 26
Curriculum Correlation 30

River
Scene 34
Background Information 35
Plants and Animal Samples 37
Living Things of the River 43
Living Things of the River Chart 49

Lakes, Ponds, Saltwater Marshes
Scene 52
Background Information 53
Plants and Animal Samples 56
Living Things of the Lakes, Ponds, Saltwater Marshes 63
Living Things of the Lakes, Ponds, Saltwater Marshes Chart 71

Valley

Scene 75
Background Information 76
Plants and Animal Samples 78
Living Things of the Valley 87
Living Things of the Valley Chart 92

Prairie

Scene 95
Background Information 96
Plants and Animal Samples 97
Living Things of the Prairie 101
Living Things of the Prairie Chart 105

Desert

Scene 108
Background Information 109
Plants and Animal Samples 110
Living Things of the Desert 115
Living Things of the Desert Chart 120

Mountains

Scene 123
Background Information 124
Plants and Animal Samples 126
Living Things of the Mountains 130
Living Things of the Mountains Chart 134

Ocean

Scene 136
Background Information 137
Plants and Animal Samples 139
Living Things of the Ocean 143
Living Things of the Ocean Chart 148

Polar Lands

Scene 151
Background Information 152
Plants and Animal Samples 154
Living Things of the Polar Lands 159
Living Things of the Polar Lands Chart 164

Literature

Literature 167

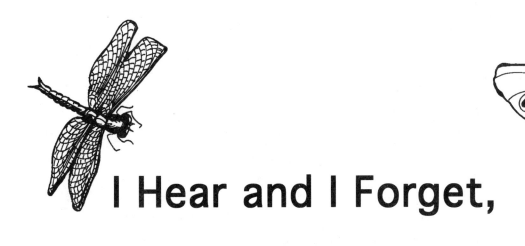

I Hear and I Forget,

I See and I Remember,

I Do and I Understand.

Chinese Proverb

Project 2061
The Living Environment
K–2 Benchmarks*

Flow of Matter and Energy

Plants and animals both need to take in water, and animals need to take in food. In addition, plants need light.

Diversity of Life

Plants and animals have features that help them live in different environments.

Cells

Most living things need water, food, and air.

Evolution of Life

Different plants and animals have external features that help them thrive in different kinds of places.

Interdependence of Life

Animals eat plants or other animals for food and may also use plants (or even other animals) for shelter and nesting.

Some animals and plants are alike in the way they look and in the things they do, and others are very different from one another.

Heredity

There is variation among individuals of one kind within a population.

Stories sometimes give plants and animals attributes they really do not have.

Offspring are very much, but not exactly, like their parents and like one another.

Living things are found almost everywhere in the world. They are somewhat different in different places.

* American Association for the Advancement of Science. *Benchmarks for Science Literacy.* Oxford University Press. New York. 1993.

Project 2061
The Living Environment
3-5 Benchmarks*

Flow of Matter and Energy

Almost all kinds of animals' food can be traced back to plants.

Some source of "energy" is needed for all organisms to stay alive and grow.

Over the whole earth, organisms are growing, dying, and decaying and new organisms are being produced by the old ones.

Interdependence of Life

For any particular environment, some kinds of plants and animals survive well, some survive less well, and some cannot survive at all.

Heredity

Some likenesses between children and parents, such as eye color in human beings, or fruit and flower color in plants, are inherited.

Insects and various other organisms depend on dead plant and animal material for food.

Evolution of Life

Individuals of the same kind differ in their characteristics, and sometimes the differences give individuals an advantage in surviving and reproducing.

Changes in an organism's habitat are sometimes beneficial and sometimes harmful.

Diversity of Life

A great variety of kinds of living things can be sorted into groups in many ways using various features to decide which things belong to which group.

Organisms interact with one another in various ways besides providing food. Many plants depend on animals for carrying their pollen to other plants or for dispersing their seeds.

Features used for grouping depend on the purpose of the grouping.

* American Association for the Advancement of Science. Benchmarks for Science Literacy. Oxford University Press. New York. 1993.

Project 2061
The Living Environment
6-8 Benchmarks*

Interdependence of Life

In all environments — freshwater, marine, forest, desert, grassland, mountain, and others — organisms with similar needs may compete with one another for resources, including food, space, water, air, and shelter. In any particular environment, the growth and survival of organisms depend on the physical conditions.

Diversity of Life

All organisms, including the human species, are part of and depend on two main interconnected global food webs. One includes microscopic ocean plants, the animals that feed on them, and finally the animals that feed on those animals. The other web includes land plants, the animals that feed on them, and so forth. The cycles continue indefinitely because organisms decompose after death to return food material to the environment.

Flow of Matter and Energy

Food provides the fuel and building material for all organisms. Plants use the energy from light to make sugars from carbon dioxide and water. This food can be used immediately or stored for later use. Organisms that eat plants break down the plant structures to produce the materials and energy they need to survive. Then they are consumed by other organisms.

Energy can change from one form to another in living things. Animals get energy from oxidizing their food, releasing some of its energy as heat. Almost all food energy comes originally from sunlight.

* American Association for the Advancement of Science. *Benchmarks for Science Literacy.* Oxford University Press. New York. 1993.

Purpose

The purpose of *Exploring Environments* is to enhance and extend the study of landforms by connecting Life Science to Earth Science. After children have had experiences with Earth studies and can identify major landforms on our Earth, a natural extension to their learning is to study the environments that are found on and near those landforms. The world has many different environments and distinct environments support different types of organisms.

In this set of explorations, students will investigate different environments as though they were taking an expedition through each. Background information, backdrop scenes, sample plants and animals, and a Science Buddy have been provided to help students examine the complex interactions between living things and how they meet their survival needs. The instructional approach is very open-ended and student-centered.

The teaching activities in this guide are divided into three grade-level spans, K – 2, 3 – 4, and 5 – 6, to allow for different foci. Each grade-level span is written for developmental appropriateness. Please use ideas from any section that you feel will work for you and your students.

Students in K – 2 focus on the characteristics of organisms. In grades 3 – 4 they learn to associate the organisms with their environment and realize organisms' dependence on the environment for resources. Students in grades 5 – 6 do more independent research to explore populations and communities of species and the ways they interact with each other and their environment.

Assessment is naturally embedded into all the activities through oral language, writing, drawing, reporting, discussing, and presenting.

Sample Science Careers

Science is an adventure that people everywhere can take part in, as they have for many centuries.

Benchmarks for Science Literacy

A **Biologist** studies the science of life in all its forms, all plants and animals. Biology is such a broad field of study that biologists usually specialize in one area.

Botanist

studies plants

Ecologist

studies relationships among living things and between organisms and their environment

Entomologist

studies insects

Exobiologist

works with astronomers to search for life elsewhere in the universe

Herpetologist

studies reptiles

Ichthyologist

studies fish

Limnologist

studies freshwater and the organisms that live there

Marine Biologist

studies life in the ocean

Microbiologist

studies organisms that can be seen only with a microscope

Ornithologist

studies birds

Wildlife Biologist

studies biology of wildlife

Zoologist

studies animals

Materials and Management Suggestions

Environmental Information

The information provided about the landforms, plants, and animals is written for teacher information in the primary grades. In the intermediate grades, this same information can be read and used by the students as a part of their independent research on the life forms and the environments of the landforms. A chart is provided for use by intermediate students when gathering their information. This same chart may be used by primary teachers to organize information before teaching. The *Living Things* text and picture pages are arranged so there is a picture with the description and classification of the living thing. The students can use the pages for information, to sort and classify the plants and animals, and to give reports about them.

Backdrop Scenes

Blackline masters are provided in this book that, when enlarged 400% and colored, can be used as backdrop scenes. However, large (17x22"), full color backdrop scenes can be purchased along with this book or purchased separately. These scenes can be laminated to last for an extended period of time. They can be used flat on a table or on a bulletin board, bent to stand up, or propped up as a stage.

If the backdrop is used as a stage, the plants and animals can be placed in front to make the scene look more three-dimensional. A toothpick can be attached to the pictures of the living things and placed in a small piece of clay or a paper stand can be made to mount on the backside of the pictures. Rocks, sand, and other Earth materials can be added in front of the stage for realism.

Older students can make their own backdrops, murals, and puppet stages from cardboard and refrigerator boxes for presentations.

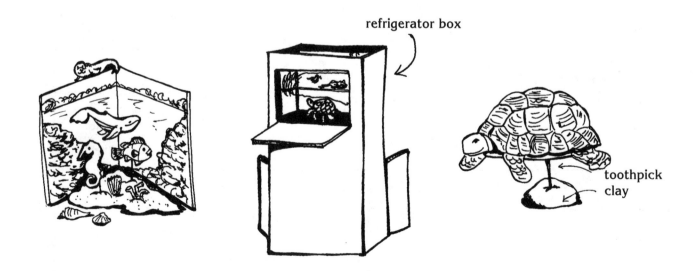

refrigerator box

toothpick
clay

Living Things Samples

Each environment has artwork samples of living things that might be found there. The plants and animals provided are but a small sample of the multitude of life forms that reside in each environment. The drawings are labeled with colors to guide you. Remember that the coloration of the actual animals may vary and that the suggested colors might not match the animals of your local region.

Many living things live in more than one environment, therefore, pictures can be used in multiple scenes. One example is the coyote which can be found in the deserts, valleys, and mountains. Extra copies of the living things can be made for other activities. Additional pictures of plants and animals can be drawn or cut from magazines to add to the environments.

Plants and animals are not drawn completely to scale, rather they are drawn to fit into the scene's foreground, midground, and background. The smallest animals and plants like insects and flowers should be placed in the foreground near the bottom of the scene (close to you). Larger organisms like trees and bison should be placed in the background, closer to the horizon line, higher on the page (farther from you).

← horizon line

← foreground

The entire presentation can be made into a puppet show by taping the Science Buddy characters and living organisms to straws or small wooden sticks.

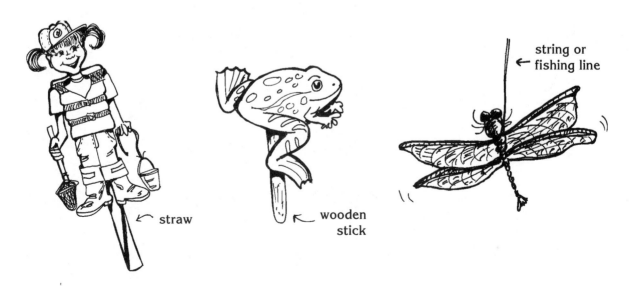

← straw

← wooden stick

string or ← fishing line

Exploring Environments
Plans and Activities — Grades K–2

What do I know?

1. Dress up as if you are going on an expedition. Have a backpack or a bag packed with your essentials. Make your imaginary stay for one day or stretch it out for a "safari week" with tent and sleeping bag props.

sunscreen · backpack · hat · water · lunch · sunglasses

2. Introduce the idea of *environment* as surroundings. Have students describe the surroundings of their classroom or their school. What kinds of living things are there and what do they need to survive? Tell your students that they are going on an imaginary journey, an adventure to an environment different from where they live. Pick an environment that many of your students may have already experienced (a lake or river) or choose one that you know will be very different from their past experiences.

3. Display the backdrop scene of the landform and review what features of the Earth are found there. If possible, have magazine pictures of the landform available for students to observe and compare to the backdrop scene.

magazine ads

4. Ask the class members to close their eyes and imagine the selected landform.
   - What do you already know about this place? (example: desert, ocean, valley)
   - What animals/plants do you think we would find in the environment?
   - Have you been to this type of environment before? If so, what did you see?
   - What is the weather like in this environment?
   - Describe how you would dress for a day/night in this environment.
   - What could cause this environment to change?

5. Have students go home and discuss with their families what plants and animals might live in the environment that you are studying. Encourage the children to write, draw, or cut out pictures of things that could live there and bring them back to school for sharing.

Developing Ideas — K–2

1. The next day, gather your students into an Expedition Team (Safari Club, Discovery Group) in front of the backdrop scene and ask them what they found out. Make a list of ideas that they bring out during discussion. Record your students' responses to the previous day's questions on a "What We Know" chart.

What We Kow About the Valley
Deer live in the valley. Blong
There is grass in the valley. Katie

2. Introduce one or more of the Science Buddies who will act as a guide to the expedition. Have students make a list of questions for the Science Buddy to answer. Record these on a class chart titled "What We Want To Know" or have children write their questions in their science journals.

crickets sing.   *The valley is flat.*

What We Want to Know About the Valley
1. What do bears eat? Tong
2. How cold is it? Lydia
3. Where do eagles live? Maddy
4. Where are the waterfalls? Marvin

3. Introduce three to five plants that live in that environment.
Use the Science Buddy stick puppet to give special facts about those plants and discuss how those plants meet their needs to stay alive. Place the plants on the scene with tape or place them in front of the scene by pushing the cutout into a small piece of clay.

4. Next, add three to five animals in the same way. Discuss how each animal meets its survival needs. Have students write and draw about the plants and animals that are introduced. Encourage them to share this new information at home.

- What does the animal eat?
- How does the animal keep itself safe?
- Where does the animal live?
- Where does the animal get its water?
- What animal might eat this animal?

eats seeds, nuts, berries — chipmunk
lives in a burrow or nest underground
sleeps in winter
eats slugs, insects, caterpillars
red-brown fur

5. Continue to add living things each day to the environment scene until it is rich with representation of life. Encourage students to find other living things to add through research and interview. Provide videos, laser discs, and library books that relate to the environment to extend and reinforce their understandings. Make the scene more realistic by adding Earth materials to it such as sand and rock for a desert scene or a tub of salt water with an "iceberg" for the Arctic. Follow the same format to teach other environments of your choice.

Application of Knowledge — K–2

After these experiences, discussions, and activities, students can show their learning in a variety of ways. These activities are valuable assessment tools that demonstrate both process and concept learning. Students can work as partners, in groups of three or four, or as individuals at a learning station task. Choose from following ideas.

1. Ask students to write or draw something they have learned. Hold an expedition discussion. Record the students' statements on a class chart "What We Learned."

2. Provide the living things cutouts in bags or boxes. Have students choose three or more of each and arrange them in a new scene they have drawn (12" x 18"). Invite them to write or dictate a story about their scene.

3. Have students make comparison charts in which they compare the traits of two or more living things.

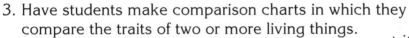

Garter Snake	Porcupine
scales	hair
no legs	4 legs
eats rodents	eats plants
reptile	mammal

chipmunk — small burrows, stores food, hides / fur, mammal, valley, plant eater / deer — large antlers, long legs for running

4. Direct students to group the animals according to their locomotion, body covering, eating habits, animal group, or some system of their choice.

Fur	Feathers	Scales

Swim	Fly	Walk	Slither

Meat eater	Plant eater	Both

5. Instruct students to arrange three or more organisms into a food chain (older students could do a food web). If using the cutouts, have the students glue the cutouts down as a record of their learning. As a final presentation, have students display their creations and tell stories about their pictures.

crow

butterfly

blue lupine

6. Have students pick one animal from the environment to study. Direct them to become an "expert" on that animal's habits. To present, have the student talk for the Science Buddy stick puppet and tell all that has been learned.

I learned that the harp seal eats fish and the polar bear hunts the seal.

7. Ask students to think about a trip to the environment studied. What would they need to take with them if they stayed a day or a week? Have students draw what they would pack to take with them. How would they get their food and water? How would they stay warm and dry? How would they see at night?

What would you pack?

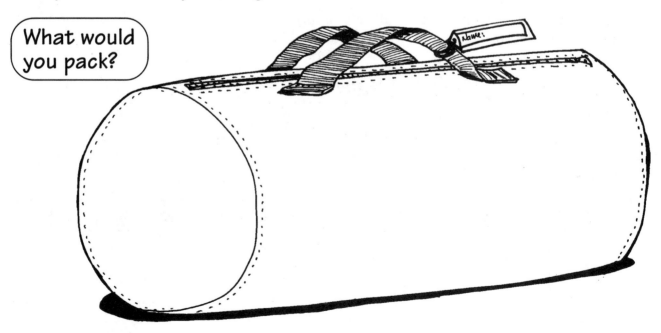

Curriculum Correlation — K-2

Language Arts

1. Use audio or video tape to record students during an imaginary camping adventure story in the environment studied.

2. Choose a few animals to make a simple food chain. Place the animals on the backdrop scene or project them on the screen with an overhead projector. Have students write or dictate sentences about the picture. Example: *The hawk tried to catch the rabbit. The rabbit hid under the rock and ate grass.*

3. Make small word cards from the pictures of plants and animals. Place the picture on the card along with the word. Have students use those words in sentence strips. When they have formed sentences, have them write the sentences in their journals.

Mathematics

1. Have students write math problems from the completed display. Example: *There are 3 prairie dogs, 1 coyote, 1 bull snake, and 2 bison in the buffalo grass. How many legs are there in all? Prove your answer.*

2. Use an overhead projector to enlarge some of the pictures to show the actual size of the animal. Have students compare the actual size of the animal to their own size.

3. Have the students compare the actual sizes of the animals. Direct the students to rank the animals in order from smallest to largest. Have them compare number of offspring for the various animals and rank them from least number of babies to most number of babies.

Art

1. Have students do a large painting of an animal on butcher paper. Direct them to make two cutouts of the animal, staple around the edges, and stuff the insides with the extra paper or newspaper. Place the animals on a bulletin board mural or hang from the ceiling.

2. Invite students to enlarge the backdrop to make a mural of one or more of the environments.

3. To reinforce the concept of camouflage, give each student an outline of one animal and have them color or decorate it so that it could blend in and be hidden somewhere in the classroom.

4. Make or buy sponges in the simple shape of an animal. Have students dip these in paint and create pictures by printing patterns.

5. Encourage students to make three-dimensional clay or paper mâché animals. Have the students place the animals in a diorama with real or cut-out plants.

Bison on Prairie by Josh

Exploring Environments
Plans and Activities — Grades 3–4

What do I know?

1. Choose an environment that you would like to use as a beginning class study. Dress the part for a hiking trip. Wear sunglasses and a hat for protection, shoes for hiking, and carry a fanny pack or backpack. Play a game in which students guess where on Earth you are planning to go. Tell them they get to ask 20 questions in order to determine where your trip (expedition or safari) will be. Inform them that they can only ask questions to which you can respond with yes or no.

2. Once they have guessed where you are going, have them sit quietly for one minute and think about that place (land, animals, plants, weather). Give them a few minutes to write or draw in their science journals. Have volunteers share their thoughts and past experiences about this environment, if applicable.

3. Use a map or magazine pictures to introduce the idea of the environment. Review what students think they know about the land of that environment. Record their input into a web that includes landforms, weather, location. Add another part to the web labeled "plants and animals." Have small groups of students brainstorm a list of plants and animals they think might live there. After about seven minutes, call the groups back to share their lists with the class. Record their ideas into the web. This activity will give you insight and help to inform you of any naive conceptions.

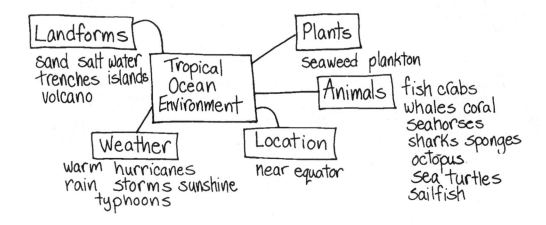

4. Have students record a list of questions in their science journals they would like answered during the course of study of this environment. Ask them to share their questions with the other members of their group and perhaps add to their own list.

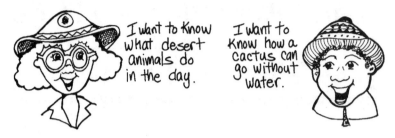

I want to know what desert animals do in the day.

I want to know how a cactus can go without water.

Developing Ideas — Grades 3–4

1. Display the backdrop scene. Identify the landforms and review what students already know about the land. Discuss the questions they wrote in their science journals yesterday. You may wish to make a class chart of questions to refer to as you teach.

2. Refer to the knowledge web the class created. Highlight the different groups to be studied: land, mammals, insects, fish, reptiles, amphibians, birds, plants, trees. Explain that the class will work together to gather information and share about this environment. Divide the class into small teams of three to five students. Inform them that each team is responsible for one area of study. To determine the environments for each group, draw cards or ask for volunteers.

land   birds   mammals   insects   reptiles   amphibians   fish   plants

3. Print the environmental and organism information along with the living things sample drawings for each group. Take a trip to the library and computer resources area to gather more information. Inform the students that the teams are expected to become "experts" in their fields of research. Tell them that their presentations can be done as puppet shows by using one or more of the Science Buddies and the living things samples as puppets. Encourage them to add music, sounds, costumes, and commercial puppets to make the presentations more interesting. Provide enough time for groups to study, draw, and practice for their presentations. An alternative presentation method is to give each child a different plant or animal to study for individual reports.

Application of Knowledge — Grades 3–4

1. At presentation time, provide the backdrop scene and have the landform group give the first presentation.

2. Following the landform presentation, have each team member come up to the environment and add the organisms to the backdrop scene as his/her learning is shared. Audience members can use the *Research Notes* chart to record facts about the organisms or to record class notes that can be put into their journals after the presentations.

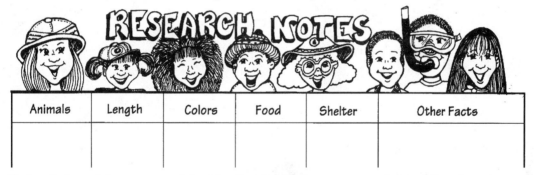

Animals	Length	Colors	Food	Shelter	Other Facts

3. Once all the living things are added to the backdrop scene, introduce the concept of food chain. Have students give you a few simple food chains (three to five links). Point out that all energy comes from the sun and that the food actually starts with plants (producers) and ends with some animal (consumer).

4. When students understand the chain idea, introduce food webs by making connections between the chains they identified. Emphasize that all the plants and animals in an environment affect each other. Have students think about and discuss the following questions:

- What happens to the balance if one animal or plant dies out?
- What happens if one plant or animal overpopulates the environment?
- What happens if the water, air, and/or ground are polluted?
- What can we do in our daily lives to help care for this environment?

5. Move on to the study of other environments and study them in the same way. Invite other classes to tour your environments and listen to Science Buddies share their knowledge, or host a science evening for parents where all environments are on display and have the children teach their parents about each one.

RESEARCH NOTES

Animals	Length	Colors	Food	Shelter	Other Facts

Curriculum Correlation — Grades 3–4

Language Arts

1. Have students do an animal report by choosing one animal from the environment. The report should include a physical description, a detailed drawing, food, predators, home, offspring, and survival skills.

2. Direct students to write a story about *A Day in the Environment* (desert, ocean, etc.). What do they see, hear, feel, do? They could write their story from the viewpoint of one of the organisms of that environment in which they become the plant or animal and describe a day in its life.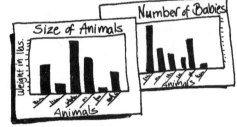

3. Encourage students to write and perform a skit about polluters in an environment. Tell them to be sure that the polluters see the error of their ways and clean up after themselves.

Mathematics

1. Have students gather data about the animals or plants and write story problems for others to solve. Example: *A mouse has four times as many offspring as a cougar. If a cougar has three babies, how many does the mouse have?*

2. Direct students to graph data about the plants and animals.

Art

1. Have students create a poster to promote environmental protection. Display the posters in the school cafeteria.

2. Direct students to draw a new backdrop scene and add organisms to it. Have them make a mural to decorate the room or a hallway at school.

3. Invite students to make paper mâché animal masks or use face paint to decorate their faces to look like animals.

A DAY in the LIFE of

By: _____

Morning

_____
_____
_____
_____

Afternoon

_____
_____
_____

Night

_____
_____
_____

Exploring Environments
Plans and Activities — Grades 5–6

What do I know?

1. Use a world map or globe to introduce the idea of environments around the world. Have small groups of students brainstorm a list of landforms that are found on Earth. After about 10 minutes, call the groups back to share their lists with the class. Record their ideas into a web.

2. If any of the major landforms are missing, point to the map or globe to help them remember. Continue with a discussion of the landforms. What do the students know about each one? Add those thoughts to the web.

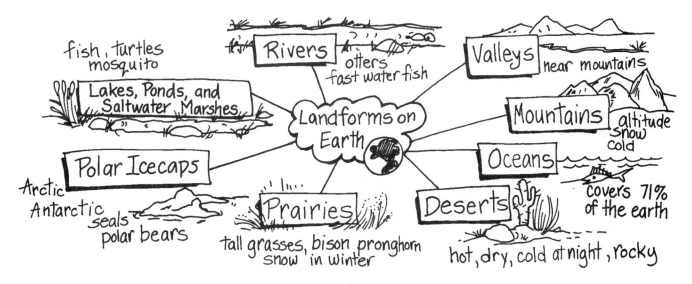

fish, turtles mosquito

Rivers — otters fast water fish

Valleys — near mountains

Lakes, Ponds, and Saltwater Marshes

Landforms on Earth

Mountains — altitude snow cold

Polar Icecaps

Oceans — covers 71% of the earth

Arctic Antarctic — seals polar bears

Prairies — tall grasses, bison pronghorn snow in winter

Deserts — hot, dry, cold at night, rocky

3. Discuss the concept of environment as surroundings. Have students describe their school environment in their science journals. What are the living and nonliving things in their environment? What are the space, conditions, and factors that affect their quality of life? How would their environment change if there were twice as many students in their class? ... half as many? What if the heating and cooling systems were broken?

Twice as many students !?!!

Broken heater !?!!

21

4. Look back to the web of Earth's landforms. Ask students to think about the environments that might be found on those landforms. Explain that each landform is the basis of resources needed for living things to survive. Each landform will have a different environment with different organisms living there. Ask students to think about which environment they would most like to study. Tell them that they will be asked to form study teams for researching and presenting projects on the various environments.

Developing Ideas — Grades 5–6

1. Assign environments to prearranged study groups or allow self-arranged study teams to volunteer for the environments to investigate and present. With great enthusiasm, tell your students that they have been selected as members of elite research scientist teams whose mission is to investigate the Earth's environments to determine their balance and health. If students have an interest in studying an environment other than deserts, oceans, icecaps, lakes, ponds, saltwater marshes, rivers, prairies, mountains, or valleys, then they can do their own research and art work.

I want to study oceans.

2. Explain that the teams are to plan presentations that communicate their findings at the World Ecology Summit. The research, art work, and presentation is expected to be equally divided among the team members. Their performance must be both informative and entertaining to the audience. It will take from one to four weeks of planning and practice, depending on how much detail you expect from your students.

3. Give each team a copy of the backdrop scene, the environmental information on plants and animals, and the sample drawings to get them started. Take a trip to the library and computer resource area to do research. Allow students to use the materials provided or to draw all their own backdrop scenes and living things. Print extra copies of the Science Buddies in case teams want to create puppet shows. Allow time each day for teams to meet, study, plan, evaluate, and practice performances.

4. Use the student page *Environmental Study* for guiding questions.
   - What features of the Earth are found in your environment?
   - Identify the living things. How do they survive in their surroundings? (food, water, shelter, protection)
   - Describe the relationships between the living things. How do the plants and animals interact to make a food chain? ... a food web?
   - What physical features do the living things have that help them to survive?
   - What pollution dangers could damage this environment and how would the living things be affected ?

5. Choose a date for the World Ecology Summit. Share presentation ideas with teams during their preparation. Inform the teams that they can implement one of the following presentation ideas or make up one of their own:
   - Television news reporter interviewing the study team
   - Performance of a skit, poem, song, or a combination of these
   - Documentary styled after National Geographic
   - Performance of an adventure story play
   - Performance of a puppet show

6. Evaluate the teams during research and presentation time based on the following criteria. Grades could be determined by a rubric or by using the points for a percentage grade. (See *Environmental Study Evaluation*.)
   - Communication of knowledge (40)
   - Evidence of cooperation of team members (15)
   - Evidence of research information (20)
   - Creativity and style of presentation (15)
   - Artistic design of display (10)

Environmental Study

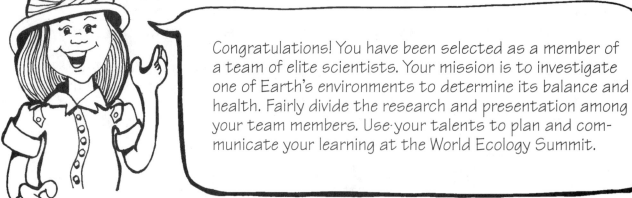

Congratulations! You have been selected as a member of a team of elite scientists. Your mission is to investigate one of Earth's environments to determine its balance and health. Fairly divide the research and presentation among your team members. Use your talents to plan and communicate your learning at the World Ecology Summit.

Names of Scientists:_____

_____

Environment: _____

Use the following questions to organize your study:

☐ 1. What features of the Earth are found in your environment?

☐ 2. Identify the living things. How do they survive in their surroundings? (food, water, shelter, protection)

☐ 3. Describe relationships between living things. How do the plants and animals interact to make a food chain? ... a food web?

☐ 4. What physical features do the living things have that help them survive in this environment?

☐ 5. What pollution dangers could damage this environment and how would they affect the organisms there?

Your team will present their findings at the World Ecology Summit. Use the information sheets, backdrop, and living things samples to create a table-top model of the environment you studied.

Environmental Study Evaluation

Environment: _____

Scientists' Names: _____   Responsibilities: _____

_____   _____
_____   _____
_____   _____
_____   _____
_____   _____

Evaluation of your research findings will take place both during your research and planning time and during your presentation session at the World Ecology Summit.

Evaluation Criteria

	My Rating	Advisor's Rating
Communication of knowledge	_____	_____
Evidence of cooperation of team members	_____	_____
Evidence of information research	_____	_____
Creativity and style of presentation	_____	_____
Artistic design of environment model	_____	_____
Total	_____	_____

What did you learn? _____

_____

How could this experience be improved? _____

_____

1. On presentation day, have teams set up displays and take turns presenting to each other. As one team presents, the audience can take notes or each team can provide a completed data sheet on the page *Research Notes*.

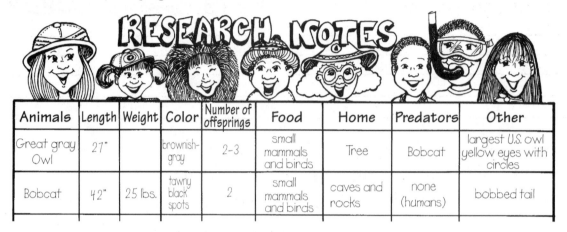

Animals	Length	Weight	Color	Number of offsprings	Food	Home	Predators	Other
Great gray Owl	27"		brownish-gray	2-3	small mammals and birds	Tree	Bobcat	largest U.S. owl yellow eyes with circles
Bobcat	42"	25 lbs.	tawny black spots	2	small mammals and birds	caves and rocks	none (humans)	bobbed tail

2. After each presentation, allow time for questions, answers, suggestions, and comments. Give students a day to improve their performances and props.

3. Have your students share their knowledge with other classrooms. Set up the displays around the edges of your room, the cafeteria, or outdoors. Invite other grade-level classes to tour the Ecology Summit. Create a schedule and have interested teachers sign up for a time slot. Divide the visiting class into groups of four or five and, on a designated signal, have them move from environment to environment and participate in the presentations. (See the invitation to the World Ecology Summit.)

4. Other ideas for sharing: Have teams go to interested classes (one or two at a time) and perform for entire classrooms or host the Ecology Summit in the evening for parents.

You are invited to the World Ecology Summit

Date: _____

Place: _____

Time: _____

Thank you for your visit. Our scientists would enjoy hearing your comments. Please write or draw about the presentations you saw.

Mountains	
Prairie	
Lakes and Ponds	
Polar Icecaps	
River	
Valley	
Oceans	
Desert	

Our scientists have taken discovery expeditions to study the world's environments. Today you have been invited to visit them at the World Ecology Summit where they present their findings.

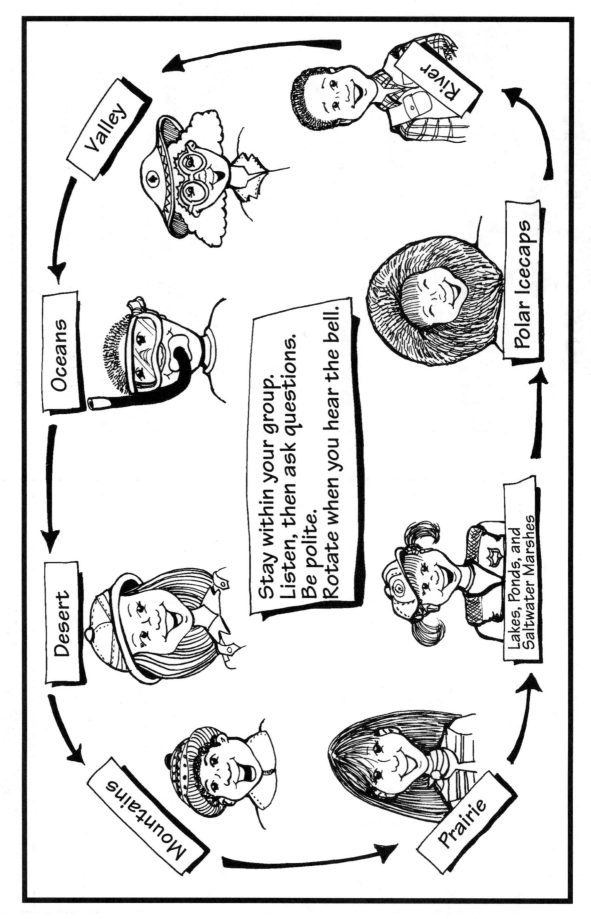

Stay within your group.
Listen, then ask questions.
Be polite.
Rotate when you hear the bell.

RESEARCH NOTES

Animals	Length	Weight	Colors	Number of offsprings	Food	Shelter	Predators	Other

Language Arts

1. Have students pretend that they are naturalists (Rangers or Science Buddies) who are going to take a tour group on a trip to an environment of their choice. Have them create an adventure story about their expedition. The planning sheet *Safari Story* can be used to guide students in the story creation.

2. Have students design and publish an *Environmental Tour* brochure. Display travel brochures and folders for ideas of design. Give the following directions:

Imagine that you are a tour guide for a sensitive environment. You are a naturalist and specialize in knowledge about this region. You take interested people on a tour through the environment that does no damage to the living things there. Members of the tour may only shoot the wildlife with cameras and video equipment. There is no interaction with the wildlife and you leave little evidence that you were there. Design an advertisement for your company that makes people want to take your tour. Tell them what they will do, what they will see, where they will stay, and what they will eat. Add pictures (drawings or photographs) and quotes from former customers. Include the cost of the tour and tips for travel to your area. Show your knowledge through your ad.

SAFARI STORY

Imagine that you are a safari leader who is going to guide a tour group on a trip to an environment of your choice. Write a story about your expedition. Use the form below to make a plan. Then weave the ideas into an interesting adventure story.

Story Setting

Location: _____

Landforms: _____

Living Things: _____

Weather: _____

Season: _____

Story Characters

Kind sad studious athletic playful shy goofy

Name: _____ Description: _____
_____

Name: _____ Description: _____
_____

Name: _____ Description: _____
_____

Name: _____ Description: _____
_____

Name: _____ Description: _____
_____

Equipment: What kinds of technology do you need?

Tools: _____

Transportation: _____

Shelter: _____

Problem: What problem will happen on this journey?

_____

_____

_____

_____

animal eats food!

plane crash

storm!

lost! injured!

Ending: How will the problem be solved?

_____

_____

_____

_____

☐ 1. Now that you have planned out a storyline, write your Safari Story rough draft. Use descriptive language so that your readers will feel they are in the environment with you.

☐ 2. Read your story out loud to yourself. ☐ 3. Make changes.

☐ 4. Share your story with a partner. ☐ 5. Listen to suggestions.

☐ 6. Make more changes. ☐ 7. Have a partner proofread.

☐ 8. Check and make changes. ☐ 9. Write your final copy.

3. Have students create a newspaper story about a natural disaster. It should be a front page story. Give the following instructions:

> Think about the environment that you have studied. Imagine that there has been a great environmental disaster — a flood, a drought, a tornado, a hurricane, a fire, a chemical spill, or air or water pollution. Write a newspaper story about the tragedy. Include the essential *who, what, where, when,* and *how* in your story. Explain the environment before and after the disaster. How does the disaster affect the living things? What can be done to help the environment return to normal?

Mathematics
1. Collect and analyze data on plants and animals. Communicate findings through graphs, Venn diagrams, and charts.

2. Write story problems for classmates to solve. Example: *A coyote can weigh 50 pounds. What fraction of a coyote's weight is a full grown black tailed rabbit ?*

3. Research reproduction rates for different animals. Assuming that all survive, how many offspring would there be in one year? ... in five years?

Art
1. Students at this age will be able to put much effort into their display through paper, clay, and paper mâché models.

2. Transform the walls of the classroom into murals from around the world.

3. Have students design and create their own puppets or masks for performances.

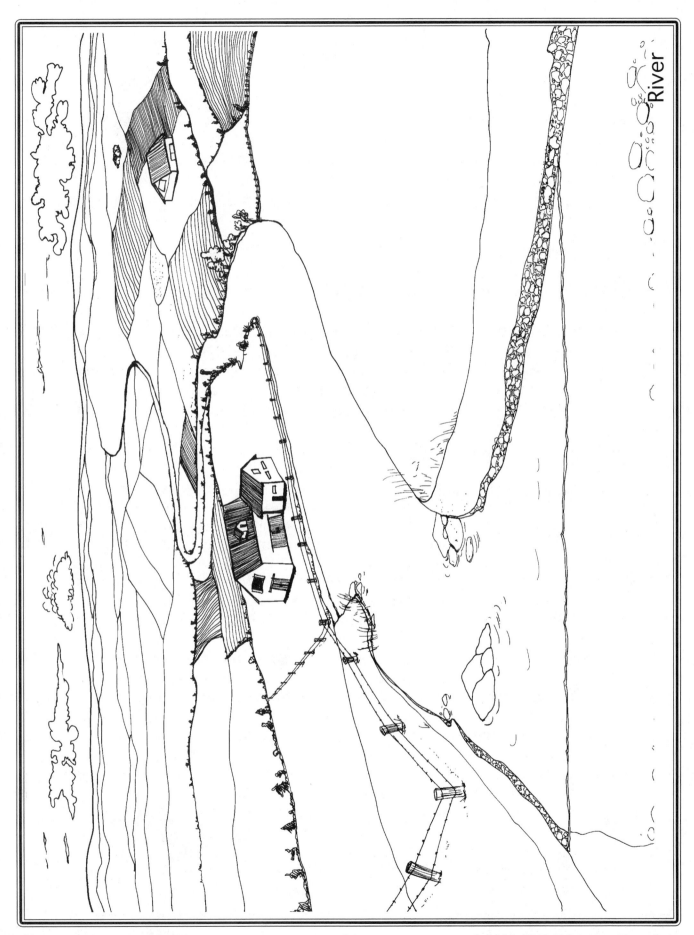

River

Rivers

A river is a natural-moving stream of fresh water. The source of the water for the rivers and streams comes from the water cycle. The moisture that has fallen on the Earth as rain or snow evaporates as water vapor. The water vapor eventually condenses and falls back to Earth as rain or snow. The water runs off or seeps into the soil and cracks in the rocks, then bubbles out as a spring further down the slope. This natural-moving flow of the water — the river — then makes it way back to the ocean and sea.

The source of a river starts in higher elevations and moves downward to lower elevations until it reaches the sea. As the water of the stream moves downward in elevation from its source, it begins to cut a channel and erode its banks. The streams of water erode the land faster upstream where the water tends to flow faster than downstream.

The upper course of a river can be very steep with the water flowing rapidly down-hill. It quite often erodes itself a deep, steep-sided, V-shaped valley. Rapids and falls can often be found here. It joins other streams, eventually growing wider and slower as it reaches the foothills and lowlands. It picks up and carries rocks, soil, and vegetation in the current, depositing them when the current slows.

As the river flows out onto the flatter land, it slows down and does not have the cutting power of the higher section. It drops some of the rocks and soil it has been carrying. The erosive power of the river eats into its banks. The sideways erosion widens the valley and the river meanders like a wriggling snake. In wide valleys, the flat area that is on both sides of the river channel is called the floodplain. It is called a floodplain because when the river is full, it will flow over its banks, and cover this area with water. When water spills out of a flooded river channel, sediment is dropped on the flooded land. These wide, flat floodplains are covered with fertile soil producing land that is suitable for raising crops.

When the river enters into a large body of water, an ocean or lake, it loses the strength of its current and can no longer carry its load of soil and dirt. It drops the sediment that was eroded along its course. The deposited sediments form a delta. When the river enters into the delta, its fresh water meets and mixes with saltwater. This mixture supports different species of plants and animals.

The river and its surrounding area are rich environments for many plants and animals, both large and small. Plants grow along the banks of the river; fish and other animals feed on them and find shelter among their roots and stems. The river otter can often be found frolicking on the banks and making slides in the mud. The weasel and the muskrat hunt among the vegetation for food. The beaver often cut down the trees along the banks of the streams to make their dens. Above the water, tall plants

35

provide hiding places and nesting locations for birds and small animals. The kingfisher makes its swift dive from an overhanging limb to spear an unsuspecting fish found in the river. High above the river hawks and eagles circle looking for their next meal of fish and other aquatic animals. The microscopic algae that float on the surface of the water provide food for insects and fish.

In almost any spot on and around large boulders found in rivers, algae, larvae, eggs, small insects and fish are found. Rocks provide an ideal hiding place for many smaller fish and animals which are hunted by larger creatures. Crayfish, snails, and clams can usually be found on the downstream side of a rock where the current is slower.

A river plays an important role in the vitality of a country. It provides a source of fresh water, transportation, recreation, protection, and food for countless living things. This is an environment that must be protected from pollution and overuse.

36

Rivers

yellow brown
with black
bands

Cottonmouth

silver

Shiners

black
back

blue gray
belly

Black Racer

sandy brown
shell

charcoal gray

Alligator Snapping
Turtle

dark olive green back
and fins

red eye

cream stomach

Largemouth
Bass

Science Buddy

Rivers

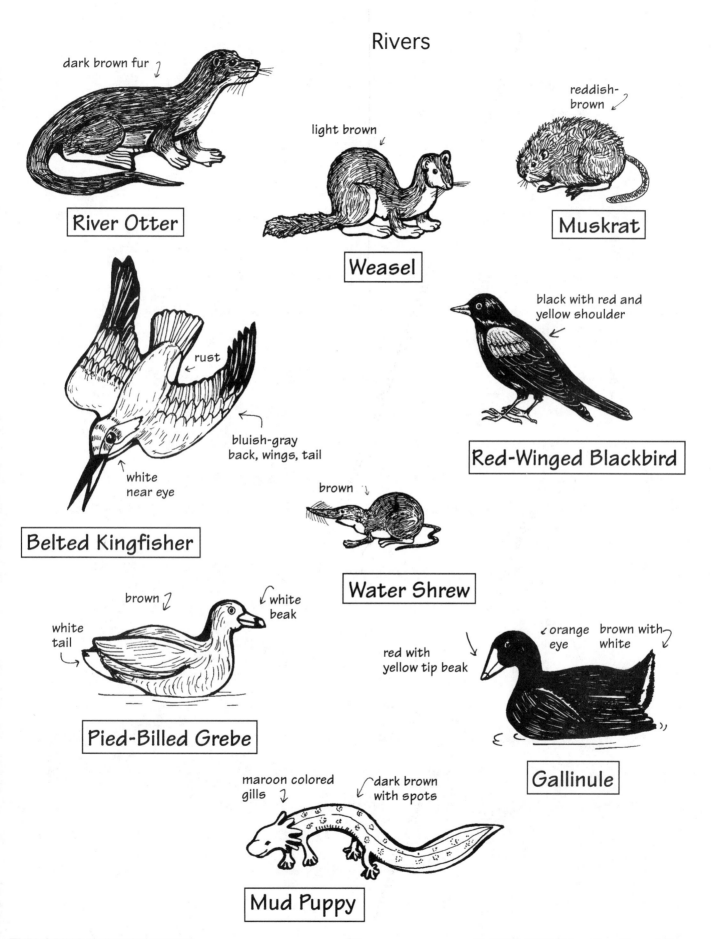

dark brown fur

River Otter

light brown

Weasel

reddish-brown

Muskrat

rust

bluish-gray back, wings, tail

white near eye

Belted Kingfisher

black with red and yellow shoulder

Red-Winged Blackbird

brown

Water Shrew

brown

white beak

white tail

Pied-Billed Grebe

orange eye

brown with white

red with yellow tip beak

Gallinule

maroon colored gills

dark brown with spots

Mud Puppy

dark brown

Water Boatman

shiny blue black

Whirligig Beetle

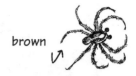
brown

Fish Spider

Diving Beetle and Larva

brown

Giant Water Bug

Black Fly and Larva

tan

Clams

greenish-tan body

Channel Catfish

tan

Snail

greenish-brown with darker spots

cream underneath

American Bullfrog

brownish-green

Tadpole

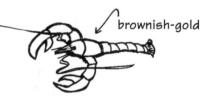
brownish-gold

Crayfish

dull gray black skin

lighter underneath

American Alligator

Rivers

green broad leaf

yellow brown leaves in fall

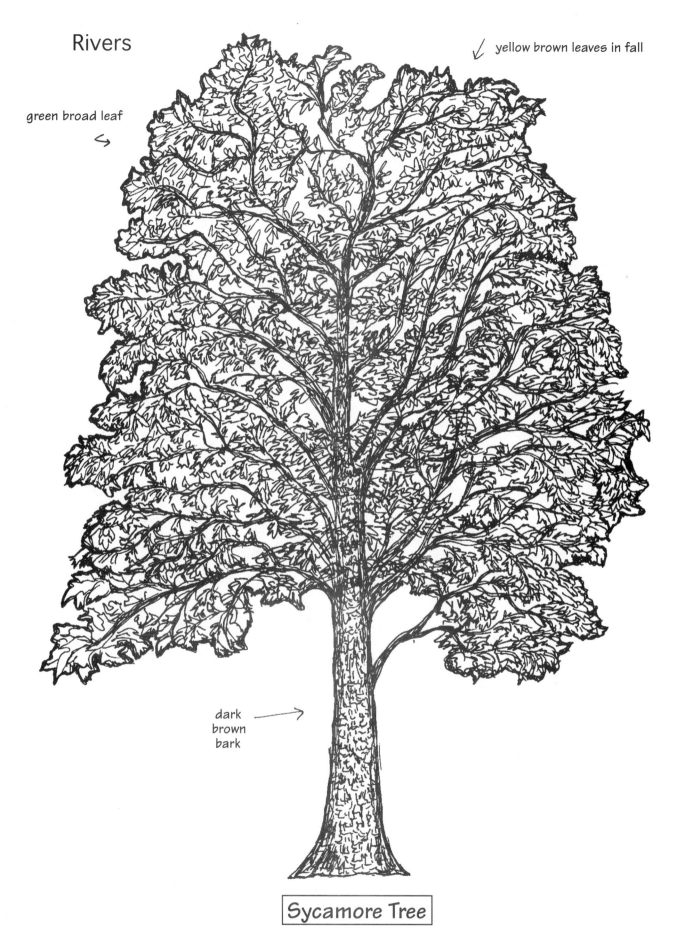

dark brown bark

Sycamore Tree

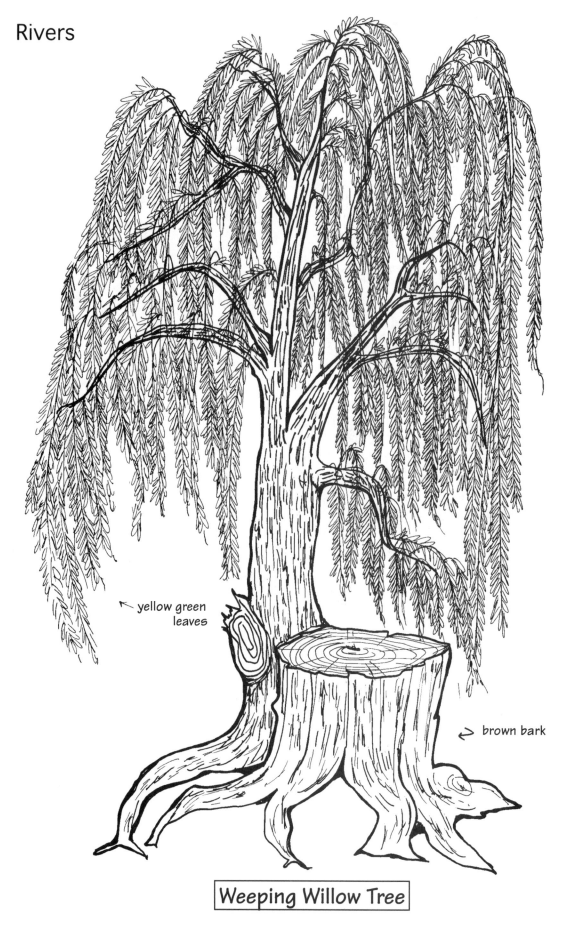

yellow green leaves

brown bark

Weeping Willow Tree

41

Rivers

white flowers ↘

yellow green leaves ↙

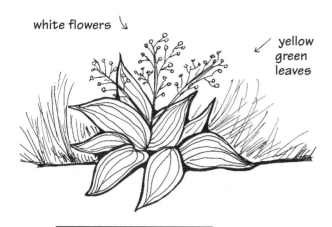

Water Plantain

pink flowers ↙

dark green leaves ↙

reddish stem ↙

Indian Balsam

purple thistle flowers

dark green leaves

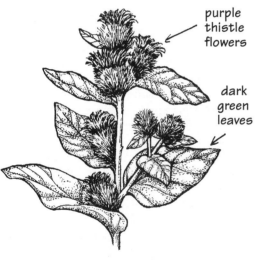

Great Burdock

yellow flowers ↙

yellow green leaves

Yellow Flag Iris

green algae on top

black fly larvae

Large River Rock

Living Things of the River

Mud Puppy   **(Amphibian)**

The mud puppy is a stubby-tailed salamander that lives in or near rivers and streams. It is 20-40 cm (8-16 in) long and has a thick brown body with dark spots. The mud puppy has feathery maroon-colored gills behind its head and its tail is flattened from side to side. It is active mainly at night when it hunts and feeds on worms, crayfish, insects, and small fish. The female mud puppy lays a hundred or more eggs. This salamander lives up to 20 years.

Black Racer   **(Reptile)**

The racer is a long, 90-190 cm (3-6 ft), slender snake. It glides swiftly along the ground, holding its head high above the surface. The black racer has a black back and a blue-gray belly. It likes to live in grassy areas and abandoned fields where it eats large insects, frogs, lizards, small rodents, and birds. The female racer lays 5-28 soft leathery eggs which hatch in six to nine weeks.

Cottonmouth   **(Reptile)**

The cottonmouth is a very poisonous snake that inhabits the rivers, swamps, ditches, and shallow lakes of southeastern United States. It is a heavy-bodied water snake, 60-190 cm (2-6 ft) long. The cottonmouth gets its name from the light "cotton" lining of its mouth which it exposes to any intruder. It preys on frogs, fish, snakes, and birds. It swims with its flat head well out of the water. The female cottonmouth gives birth every other year to 1-15 young. It has a yellow brown body with black bands.

Alligator Snapping Turtle   **(Reptile)**

A large gray turtle with a sandy brown shell, the alligator snapping turtle is the world's largest freshwater turtle. It weighs up to 90 kg (200 lbs) and is 34-65 cm (14-26 in) in length. It has three knobby ridges on its shell and a long tail. This turtle has a big head with a hooked beak which it uses to capture fish, snails, and mussels. The alligator snapping turtle has an unusual feature in its mouth, a pink worm-like projection on its tongue which it wiggles as bait to attract its food. The alligator snapping turtle is an omnivore; it eats fish, reptiles, birds, other small aquatic animals, and also feeds on the plants that grow along the river. The female alligator snapping turtle lays 10-50 round white eggs. The turtle can live up to 60 years.

American Alligator   **(Reptile)**

The American alligator is the largest reptile in North America. It lives in the rivers, swamps, bayous, and other freshwater habitats of the southern states. The alligator prowls the waterways with only its eyes and snout showing above the water. It feeds by sneaking up under water on its prey and grabbing it. It eats birds, turtles, fish, and small mammals. A large gray black animal, it grows to 2-5 m (6-15 ft) in length. The female alligator builds a mound-shaped nest of mud, leaves, and rotting organic material and deposits 25-60 eggs in it. As the mound of vegetation decays, it gives off heat that keeps the eggs warm until they hatch two to three months later. The female alligator guards the eggs until they hatch and cares for the young for a year. The alligator has a lifespan of up to 50 years.

Living Things of the River

American Bullfrog   (Amphibian)

The largest frog in the country, the American bullfrog grows to a length of 20 cm (8 in). Found in the brushy, weedy areas along the rivers, the bullfrog eats small fish, insects, small mammals such as mice, and snakes. It is a greenish-brown color with darker spots. The bullfrog gets its name from its powerful call, which sounds like the bellow of a bull. The bullfrog's strong hind legs enable it to jump long distances. Many humans catch the bullfrog because they enjoy the taste of this frog's legs. The bullfrog lays 10,000-20,000 eggs which hatch in 4-20 days. The immature stage of the bullfrog is called a **tadpole.** A tadpole can usually be found in the warmer, shallow water near the shoreline of rivers and lakes. It eats algae, bacteria, and dead fish found in the water.

Channel Catfish   Fish)

The channel catfish can grow from 5-100 cm (2-40 in) in length. A greenish-tan fish, it is easily recognized by the four pairs of feelers attached to its lower jaw. These feelers are very sensitive whisker-like appendages called barbels that are used to forage for food on the bottom of the river. A catfish has a large head, and a smooth, scaleless skin. It feeds on fish and other small water animals.

Largemouth Bass   (Fish)

A dark olive green, "hungry" game fish best describes this fish. The largemouth bass is common in rivers and lakes throughout the country. It can grow from 5-60 cm (2-24 in) in length and average 1-2 kg (2-4 lb) in weight; however, in the southern part of United States it can grow even larger. It preys on smaller fish and other aquatic animals. Humans delight in hooking these largemouth bass on their fishing lines.

Shiners   (Fish)

A shiner is a small silver fish that lives in cool, clear rivers and streams. It will usually be found gathered with many others of its kind. Its food consists largely of algae and tiny animals. This fish is commonly used as bait and as a food fish in fish hatcheries. It grows to a length of 15-20 cm (6-8 in).

River Otter   (Mammal)

The river otter is a fairly large, slender, playful animal. It spends a lot of time swimming in rivers or streams, but can get around very well on land. The nose and eyes of the otter are located high on the head so it can swim, see, and breathe while hunting in the water. Early trappers killed many otters for their thick brown pelts. An otter is about 50-90 cm (20-35 in) long, with a tail 25-50 cm (10-20 in) long. The river otter is often found rolling, sliding, diving, or frolicking on the banks of rivers and streams. It feeds mainly on fish, but also will eat mice, frogs, and crayfish. The female has one to five young. The river otter can live up to 16 years.

Living Things of the River

	Water Shrew (Mammal) A shrew looks somewhat like a mouse but has a long, slender, pointed snout, small eyes and ears. A water shrew lives along streams or in the mosses along lakes. The female has 3-10 babies that live two to three years. It eats insects and their larvae, but also consumes other invertebrates. This very small animal is 7-10 cm (3-4 in) long. It has dark, velvety brown fur. Its enemies are mink, weasels, and large fish.
	Weasel (Mammal) The weasel is a long-bodied, short-legged animal. It is 28-55 cm (11-22 in) in length and has light brown fur. The female weasel has three to nine babies a year. The weasel lives in rock piles, under tree stumps, or in abandoned rodent burrows. It is valuable in controlling populations of mice, voles, snakes, and squirrels, but it also attacks rabbits, poultry, and birds. The weasel in turn is preyed upon by owls, hawks, foxes, and cats. It can usually be found in brushy or open areas near water.
	Muskrat (Mammal) The muskrat is a large rodent with dark, glossy reddish-brown fur. It is about 30 cm (1 ft) long. It has a long tail that it uses to steer itself in the water. The female muskrat has five to six young that will live about three years. The muskrat digs its home in the banks of a stream or river, or it will build a house similar to the beaver's but made out of grasses and sedges. It tows its food out to a feeding platform to eat. The muskrat eats mostly water plants such as cat-tails, sedges, rushes, and weeds along with some land plants. It also eats snails, clams, frogs, and fish. Raccoons and mink are the muskrat's main enemies.
	Kingfisher (Bird) The kingfisher is a large-headed bird with a shaggy crest and a heavy, sharp-pointed bill. It lives on fish. It sits on a favorite spot overlooking a stream or lake hunting for fish. It will leave its perch and plunge into the water after its prey. The bird stabs the fish, beats it until it is dead, and then swallows it head first. A kingfisher usually nests in a burrow in a steep bank near water where it lays five to eight white eggs. It is a bluish-gray bird that is 29-36 cm (11-14 in) long.
	Pied-Billed Grebe (Bird) The pied-billed grebe is a small drab brown bird with a thick, short bill, lobed toes, and water-proofed feathers. It is 30-38 cm (12-15 in) long. The grebe can be found in marshes and ponds. It has the ability to sink underwater by forcing air out of its feathers and body. It will often swim with just the head and neck visible above the water's surface. It eats fish, tadpoles, and newts. The female grebe lays five to seven eggs in a large floating nest of marsh plants anchored to protective vegetation.

Living Things of the River

Gallinule   (Bird)

The gallinule is a dark brown, plump bird found in the weedy edges of rivers, lakes, and ponds. It feeds on mosquitoes, spiders, tadpoles, insect larvae, fruits, and seeds. It is 30-37 cm (12-14 in) in length. It can be recognized by its yellow-tipped red bill and greenish feet with enormously long toes. It swims well with a characteristic pumping motion of the head. It can also walk on the floating lily pads. The female gallinule lays 9-12 buff-colored eggs in a nest built of rushes at the waters edge.

Red-Winged Blackbird   (Bird)

The red-winged blackbird's red and yellow shoulders make it very noticeable in the reeds along the river where it nests. It is a black-colored bird that is 18-25 cm (7-10 in) long. The red-winged blackbird is considered a pest by farmers because it consumes grain from their fields; however, it also eats many of the harmful insects that infest their crops. It lays three to five pale blue green eggs in a woven cup located in tall weeds. It gathers in large flocks in the fall and spring.

Fish Spider   (Spider)

The fish spider is a small brown spider that runs across the surface of the water hunting for insects and small animals. It has water repellent hairs on its body that trap air. It can dive underwater for up to 45 minutes breathing the air trapped in its body hairs. The fish spider is 1-2 cm (0.5 in) long.

Diving Beetle   (Insect)

The diving beetle is found in rivers, streams, and ponds throughout most of the country. Its smooth oval body is dark brown or black and 2-4 cm (1-1.5 in) in length. It swims by flexing its hind legs together like oars. It can remain underwater for a long time breathing trapped air. It eats small fish, tadpoles, and insect larvae. The **diving beetle larva** is called a water tiger. It has strong jaws and attacks prey larger than itself.

Whirligig Beetle   (Insect)

This beetle can be found in freshwater ponds and streams, skating across the surface looking for small insects and their larvae. It is named for its habit of swimming rapidly in circles. It is an oval, black beetle 3-15 mm (less than 1 in) long. It has two long front legs which it uses to catch food and four shorter hind legs which are used to propel the beetle through the water. It feeds mainly on mosquitoes but also eats other insects and their larvae.

Water Boatman   (Insect)

The water boatman is a long, oval, brown bug that has long hind legs that are flattened for swimming. The front legs are short. Quite often it can be found clinging to submerged plants. It feeds on algae or decaying plant and animal material. The water boatman is about 2.5 cm (1 in) in length.

Living Things of the River

	Giant Water Bug (Insect) The giant water bug grows to a length of 7 cm (2.5 in). This large, brown, oval bug has front legs like claws that it uses to grasp its prey. It is so large it can feed on small fishes and tadpoles. It kills its prey with a poison secreted as it bites.
	Black Fly (Insect) The black fly is a small fly that is 1.3 cm (0.5 in) in length. It is common near streams and rivers. The female black fly is a blood-sucker, and its bite is painful. The black fly larvae can often be seen on the top and sides of rocks in rivers.
	Crayfish (Crustacean) A crayfish is often called a "freshwater lobster" because it looks like a miniature lobster. It is a mottled brownish-gold color and is 5-12 cm (2-5 in) long. It is a scavenger that is active at night when it eats food which consists of plant material and small animals.
	Snail (Mollusk) The snail lives in rivers, streams, and lakes, feeding primarily on plants. It typically has a single coiled shell. It crawls on a thick muscular foot on the underside of its body. Many different kinds of fish, birds, and other animals find snails good to eat.
	Clams (Mollusk) Clams live in the mud and sand of rivers, lakes, and streams. They are abundant in the shallower stretches of the rivers. Clams dig in the mud with their wedge-shaped foot. They have a bivalve shell. Water passes in and out of the shell through siphons. They eat algae. Many kinds of fish and animals, such as mink, raccoons, and turtles eat the clams.

Living Things of the River

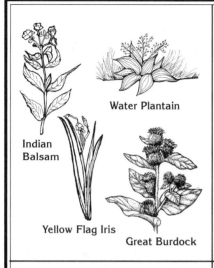

Water Plantain

Indian Balsam

Yellow Flag Iris

Great Burdock

Wildflowers   (Wildflower)

Many flowering plants can be found along the banks of the rivers. The **water plantain** can be found in shallow water and wet ground near the rivers. It grows 10-100 cm (4-36 in) tall and has white flowers on the tips of branching stalks. The leaves are oval to heart-shaped. The **yellow flag iris** roots in the mud of the riverbanks. It has a thick spreading underground stem. Its yellow blooms can be seen in early summer on 51- 90 cm (2-3 ft) stalks. The **great burdock** has purple thistle-shaped flowers blooming on stalks 30-150 cm (1-5 ft) tall. The dark green, heart-shaped leaves are large. The hooks on the seeds catch the fur of animals that pass by thus assuring the seeds will be spread widely. The **Indian balsam** is a tall water-loving plant that grows on the banks of rivers. It has pink flowers and dark green leaves. The seed cases burst at a touch and scatter the seeds in all directions.

Sycamore Tree   (Tree)

The sycamore tree lives in the river bottomlands in rich moist soil. It grows 25-30 m (80 to 100 ft) tall. This is a wide-spreading deciduous tree that is valuable for preventing erosion along the river banks. It has a reddish-brown trunk and large broad leaves. The fruit is a small brown ball which hangs from drooping stems.

Weeping Willow Tree   (Tree)

The weeping willow belongs to a large family of trees that thrives in wet soils. It is well known for its distinctive "weeping" (drooping) foliage. The soft, slender branches are used to make baskets and furniture. The roots interlace to form a network that holds the soil and prevents erosion. It has long, narrow, yellow-green leaves. It can grow 10-12 m (30-40 ft) tall.

Living Things of the River

Living Things	Home	Food	Characteristics
Amphibians			
Mud Puppy	Banks of streams, rivers	Small aquatic animals	Thick bodied, stubby-tailed salamander; dark maroon gills behind head; active at night; 20-40 cm (8-16 in)
American Bullfrog	Rivers, streams	Small fish, insects, mice, snakes	Largest frog; greenish-brown color; strong hind legs; loud call; 20 cm (8 in)
Reptiles			
Black Racer	Woods, grassy and brushy areas	Insects, frogs, lizards	Slim black body; glides swifly along ground; holds head high above surface; 90-190 cm (3-6 ft)
Cottonmouth	Swamps, streams, ditches	Frogs, fish, birds	Venomous snake; dark heavy body; large head; mouth white on inside; swims with head out of the water; 60-190 cm (2-6 ft)
Alligator Snapping Turtle	Freshwater	Fish, snails, mussels	Large freshwater turtle; big head; hooked beak; wiggles pink projectile on tongue as bait; 90 kg (200 lbs); 34-65 cm (14-26 in)
American Alligator	Rivers, swamps, bayous	Fish, turtles, birds, small mammals	Freshwater reptile; female guards eggs until they hatch and cares for young for a year; 2-5 m (6-15 ft)
Fish			
Channel Catfish	Muddy bottom of river	Fish, larvae, insects	Greenish-tan; large head; smooth, scaleless skin; 5-100 cm (2-40 in)
Largemouth Bass	Rivers, lakes	Small fish, larvae	Popular sport fish; dark green; 1-2 kg (2-4 lb); 5-60 cm (2-24 in)
Shiners	Rivers, streams	Algae, larvae	Small silver fish; often used as bait; 15-20 cm (6-8 in)

Living Things of the River

Living Things	Home	Food	Characteristics
Mammals			
River Otter	Rivers, streams, lakes	Fish, mice, frogs	Dark brown animal; wrestles, slides, plays tag, swims with other otters; 50-90 cm (20-35 in) with 25-50 cm (10-20 in) tail
Water Shrew	Streams, lake shores	Insects, mice, larvae	Long dark brown body with long pointed nose; 7-10 cm (3-4 in)
Weasel	Near water	Rats, mice	Long body; short legs; light brown fur with lighter underside; 28-55 cm (11-22 in)
Muskrat	Marshes, ponds, streams	Aquatic plants, snails	Reddish-brown rodent; lives in the banks of streams and ponds; 30 cm (1 ft)
Birds			
Kingfisher	Lakes, streams	Fish	Large blue gray bird with shaggy chest; heavy sharp bill; dives into water for fish; 29-36 cm (11-14 in)
Pied-Billed Grebe	Rivers, ponds	Fish, tadpoles	Small brown bird; thick, short bill; swims with head and neck out of water; 30-38 cm (12-15 in)
Gallinule	Edges of rivers and lakes	Spiders, mosquitoes, larvae, tadpoles	Brown bird; yellow-tipped red bill; greenish feet; long toes; walks on floating lily pads; 30-37 cm (12-14 in)
Red-Winged Blackbird	Ponds, rivers	Insects, seeds	Blackbird with red and yellow patches on shoulders; nests in the reeds along river and stream banks; 18-25 cm (7-10 in)

Living Things of the River

Living Things	Home	Food	Characteristics
Spiders and Insects			
Fish Spider	Quiet water	Insects, larvae	Small brown spider; runs on surface of water; traps air to breathe underwater; 1-2 cm (0.5 in)
Diving Beetle	Rivers, streams	Small fish, larvae, tadpoles	Dark brown oval body; swims by flexing hind legs as oars; breathes trapped air; 2-4 cm (1 in)
Whirligig Beetle	Freshwater ponds	Mosquitoes, insects	Swims rapidly in circles; uses two front legs to catch food; 3-15 mm (less than 1 in)
Water Boatman	Rivers	Algae	Long, oval, brown insect; 2.5 cm (1 in)
Giant Water Bug	Rivers	Small fish, tadpoles	Large insect; kills prey with poison; front legs like claws; large insect, 7 cm (2.5 in)
Black Fly	Streams, rivers	Sucks blood from animals	Black; larvae often found on top of river rocks; 1.3 cm (0.5 in)
Crustaceans and Mollusks			
Crayfish	Streams, rivers	Small animals, plants	Often called freshwater lobster; brownish-gold color; 5-12 cm (2-5 in)
Snail	Rivers, streams	Plants, algae	Single, coiled shell; crawls on muscular foot; tan color
Clam	Rivers	Algae	Bivalve shell; digs in mud with foot; eaten by fish and mammals
Trees			
Sycamore Tree	River banks		Deciduous tree; roots prevent erosion; 25-30 m (80-100 ft)
Weeping Willow	River banks		Yellow-green leaves on slender, drooping branches; used for baskets and furniture; 10-12 m (30-40 ft)

51

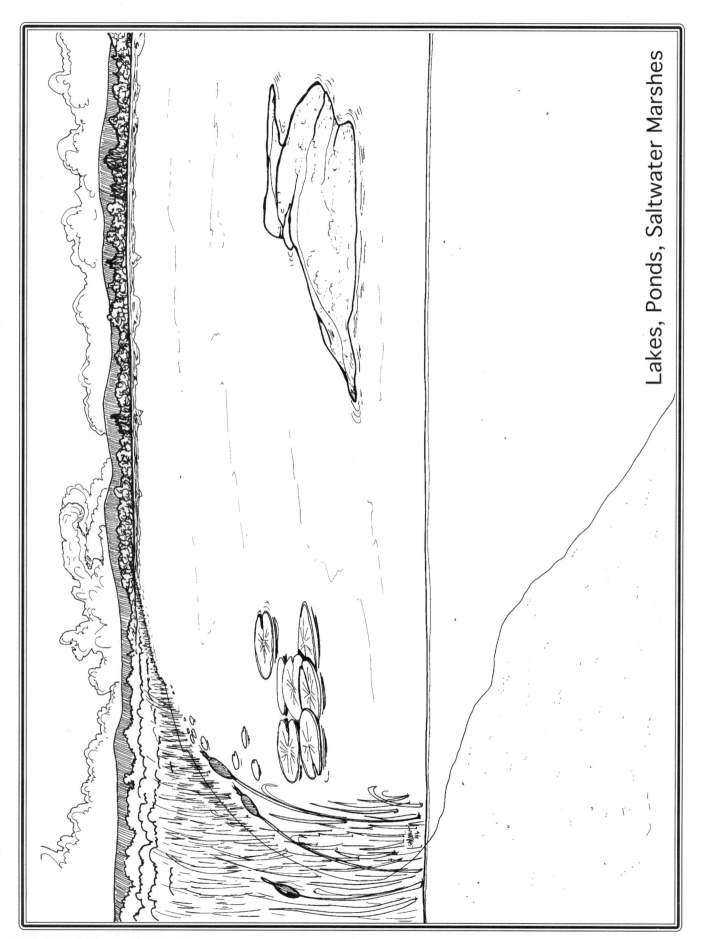

52

Lakes, Ponds, and Saltwater Marshes

Lakes

A lake or a pond is a body of water completely surrounded by land. Lakes can be found in all parts of the world. They come in all shapes and sizes. Some are so big that they are considered to be inland seas such as the huge Great Lakes of the United States. The word *lake* comes from a Greek word meaning hole or pond.

Lakes are usually deep depressions in the crust of the Earth that have filled with fresh water. Rain, melting snow, water from springs, rivers, and surface runoff fill these depressions. Most lakes have a river that enters and leaves, so water flows through the lake, in one end and out the other. Water also circulates within a lake, especially near its surface where the sun's rays warm the water.

Occasionally lakes will form in a depression where there is no outlet for the water. The Great Salt Lake is an example. There the mineral salts build up because of evaporation and the water becomes salty.

The largest number of lakes lie in regions that were once covered by glaciers. In many mountains, the glacial ice carved deep valleys. The basins that were created filled with water. On land that was flatter, glaciers gouged hollows and deposited rock and soil as they melted. Many lakes formed in the hollows and holes that were created by the glacial deposits. Sometimes lakes are formed by rainwater filling up the crater of an extinct volcano. Crater Lake in Oregon is a good example of this type of lake.

Lakes can form in regions where limestone underlies the soil. Underground water slowly dissolves the limestone rock. When the surface collapses, a sinkhole will develop and fill with water, forming beautiful crystal clear lakes.

Many artificial lakes have been formed by building dams across rivers to control the runoff of water. These dams are built for several reasons: to protect the surrounding area from floods, to provide a source of water for drinking and irrigation, to provide water to generate electricity, and for recreation. Small artificial ponds and lakes can form in gravel pits or quarries when rainwater collects in the hole left after the material has been removed.

The presence of a large body of water in an area influences the climate around it. Lake water does not warm up as fast as the surrounding land area, so breezes across the lake cool the land around it. In the winter, the lakes retain heat longer than the land, causing the climate around it to be warmer.

The economic uses of lakes are numerous. Some of the larger lakes are used as travel and trade routes. Raw materials and other products are carried by boats across the lakes to industrial centers. Lakes provide an important source of water for irrigation. They are a natural reservoir of water for communities. Lakes created as storage reservoirs can be used to generate electric power. People use lakes for a variety of recreational activities such as swimming, boating, fishing, and water skiing.

The depth of a lake helps to determine what plants and animals live in it. Shallow lakes where sunlight can reach into their deepest parts are rich in water plant life and small animals. Deep lakes quite often have a layer of cold water at the bottom which may not contain enough food or vegetation to support many forms of life. These cold, clear lakes are shunned by birds and other animal life.

Ponds

A pond can be described as a small shallow body of water. It usually has a mud bottom and plants line the shores. The temperature of the water usually remains about the same from top to bottom and changes more rapidly than larger bodies of water as the air temperature changes.

In cold northern climates, a pond can freeze over completely in the winter. Some animals still move about under the ice, but others hibernate in the mud of the pond bottom.

A lake or pond provides a very rich and varied wildlife habitat. The plants and animals in and around the area depend on one another for their survival. Water plants live on and under the surface of the water. Some are attached to the pond bottom and others float free. Water-loving plants line the shores. These plants provide food and protection for insects, snails, turtles, and fish. Waterfowl such as ducks and geese live near the water and feed on the insects and smaller animals. Larger animals use the ponds and lakes for drinking water and a source of food.

Ponds are home to many animals that live in water when they are young, such as tadpoles and the larvae of mayflies. Their later lives are spent near the water but on dry land.

In the spring there is fresh newness around a pond. Plants blossom and eggs are laid. The dense plant growth gives safe, sheltered nesting sites. In the summer, plants begin to grow. New hatchlings eat and grow, fattening up and changing. In the fall things begin to slow down; some animals leave, others visit, seeds are spread, plants dry up. In the winter, cold-blooded animals slow down and perhaps stop. There is an abundance of oxygen in the water as the water is colder. The water is rich in nutrients. Ice forms on the surface of the pond which helps to trap heat, keeping the water underneath warmer.

Saltwater Marshes

Saltwater marshes cover millions of acres along all three coasts of the United States, but they are much more common along the Atlantic Ocean and Gulf of Mexico. Saltwater marshes are found in areas where the water calms enough to drop its load of sediments. This is land that is exposed to large scale changes in temperature, salinity, and water levels. These things make the salt marsh one of the most dynamic and important, and certainly the most naturally productive, lands on Earth.

Salt marshes are found in many different places: the delta areas of river systems, along the seashore, and mud flats of an estuary. Although salt marshes are protected from the direct wave action of the tides, they are strongly influenced by the cycles of the tides. In a matter of a few hours, the tides push water in and out of these land areas and the animals and plants in this zone must shift from an aquatic environment to a terrestrial environment, then back again in a continuous cycle. This system cycles nutrients to support food chains that produce 95 percent of commercially valuable fish and shellfish in the ocean.

At the heart of the salt marsh is cord grass. Cord grass is one of the few flowering plants that can survive in saltwater. Cord grass is not only an extremely productive plant, but it also provides protective coverage for larval, juvenile, and adult life cycle stages for numerous marine organisms. Glassworts, marsh lavender, and sea oxeye are some of the plants that can withstand the salty soils.

The marsh smells rather pungent at low tide. This smell, however, is normal. The marsh mud is an oxygen-poor environment where anaerobic bacteria live. These bacteria give off hydrogen sulfide, producing a rotten-egg smell.

Salt marshes are important areas for wildlife. The numerous plants that live there provide rich nutrients for many animals that call this home. Reeds and reed beds provide food and shelter for many birds, fish, crabs, shrimp, and frogs. The water of the wetlands is also a breeding ground for many insects. These wetlands can be the spawning grounds for fish, lobsters, and shrimp. Terns, skimmers, egrets, and herons can be seen feeding in the salt marsh. The borders of the salt marsh provide homes for raccoons, rabbits, and marsh rats.

In the past, marshlands were considered wastelands, useless unless drained and developed. Now people have come to realize these lands play an important role in the ecology of the Earth. Animals and humans benefit from the thousands of acres of marshlands in North America. They are part of the National Wildlife Refuge system and are protected for use as breeding grounds and stopover areas for ducks and other waterfowl populations. Larger animals visit the marshlands in search of food and water.

Lakes, Ponds, Saltwater Marshes

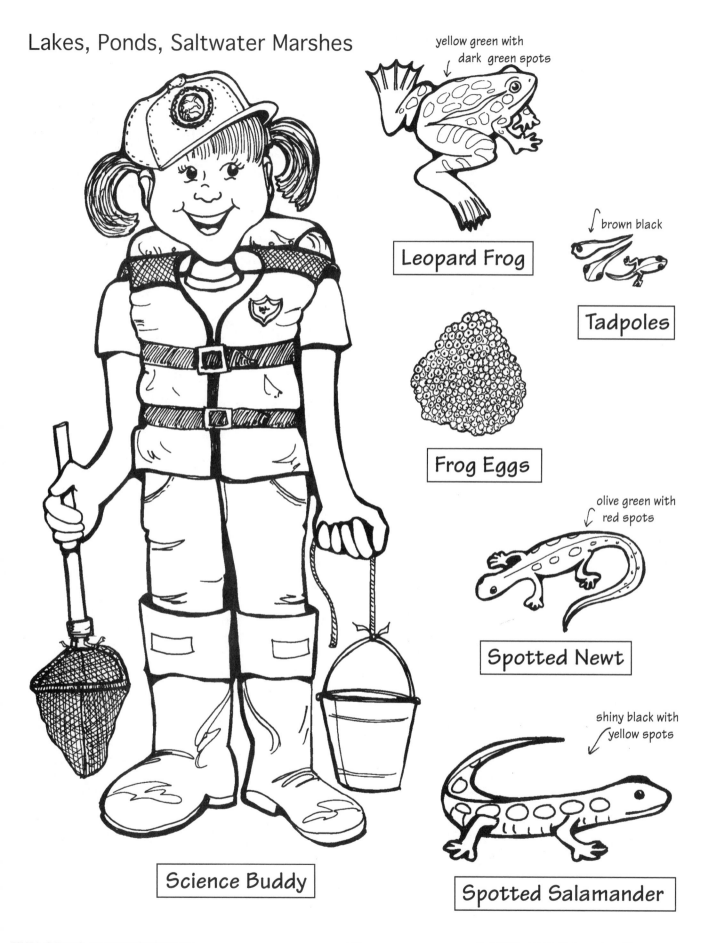

yellow green with
dark green spots

Leopard Frog

brown black

Tadpoles

Frog Eggs

olive green with
red spots

Spotted Newt

shiny black with
yellow spots

Science Buddy

Spotted Salamander

Lakes, Ponds, Saltwater Marshes

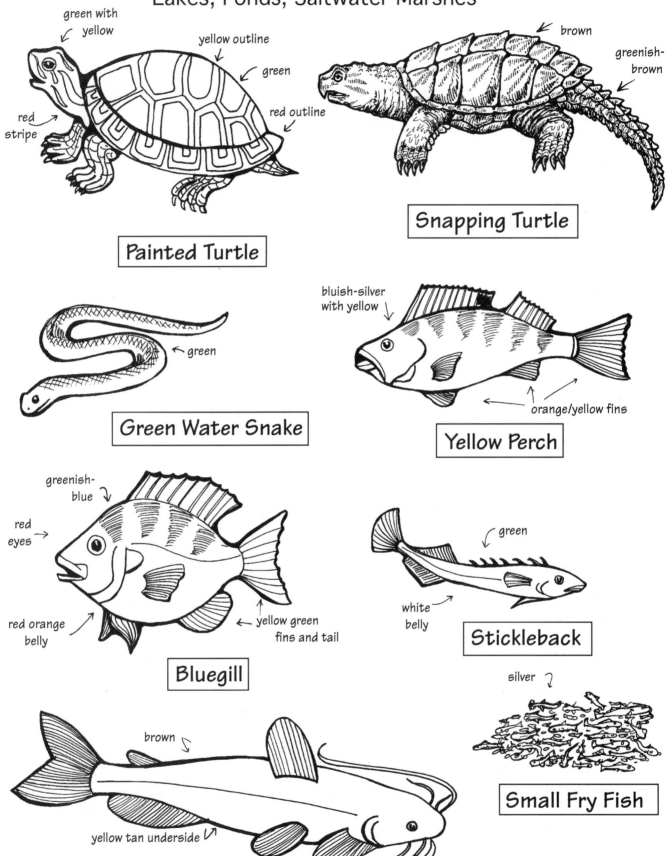

green with yellow

yellow outline

green

red stripe

red outline

brown

greenish-brown

Snapping Turtle

Painted Turtle

green

bluish-silver with yellow

orange/yellow fins

Green Water Snake

Yellow Perch

greenish-blue

red eyes

red orange belly

yellow green fins and tail

green

white belly

Stickleback

Bluegill

silver

brown

yellow tan underside

Small Fry Fish

Catfish

Lakes, Ponds, Saltwater Marshes

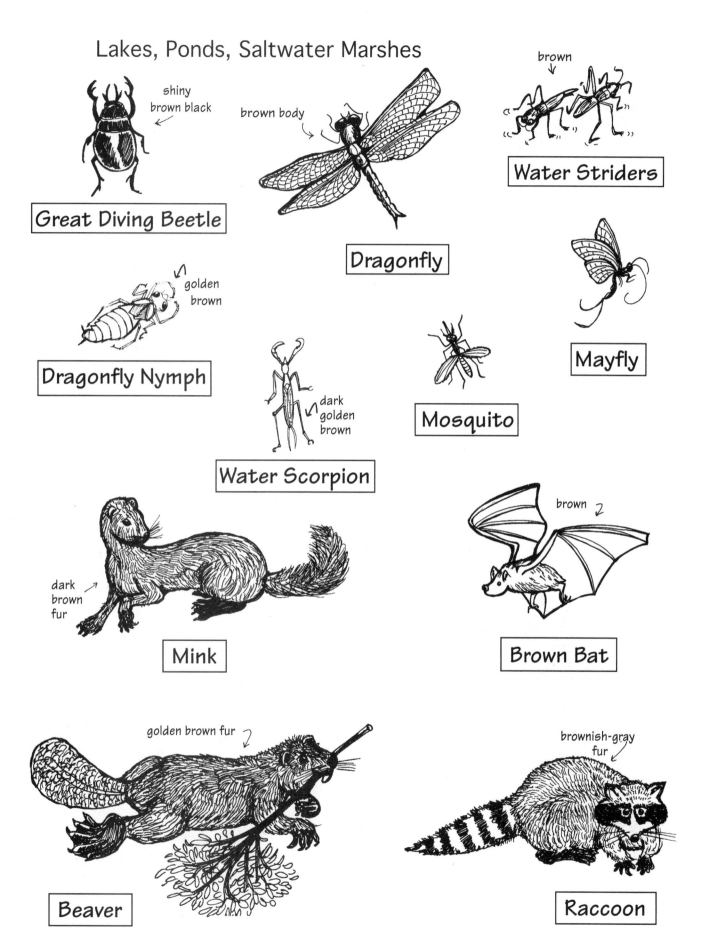

shiny brown black

Great Diving Beetle

brown body

Dragonfly

brown

Water Striders

golden brown

Dragonfly Nymph

dark golden brown

Water Scorpion

Mosquito

Mayfly

dark brown fur

Mink

brown

Brown Bat

golden brown fur

Beaver

brownish-gray fur

Raccoon

Lakes, Ponds, Saltwater Marshes

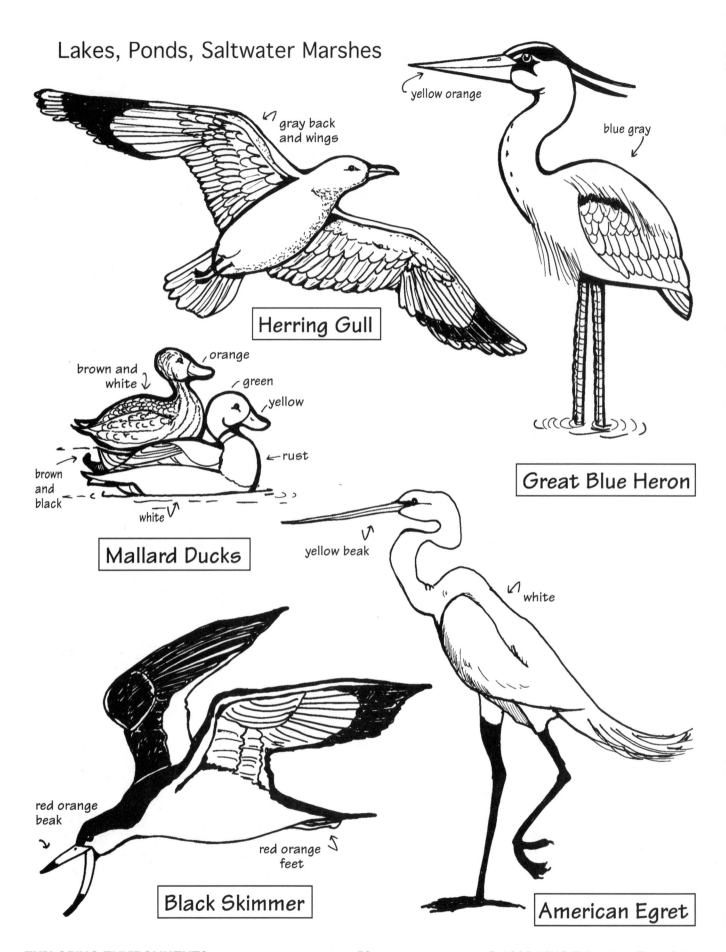

gray back and wings

Herring Gull

yellow orange

blue gray

Great Blue Heron

brown and white

orange

green

yellow

rust

brown and black

white

Mallard Ducks

yellow beak

white

red orange beak

red orange feet

Black Skimmer

American Egret

Lakes, Ponds, Saltwater Marshes

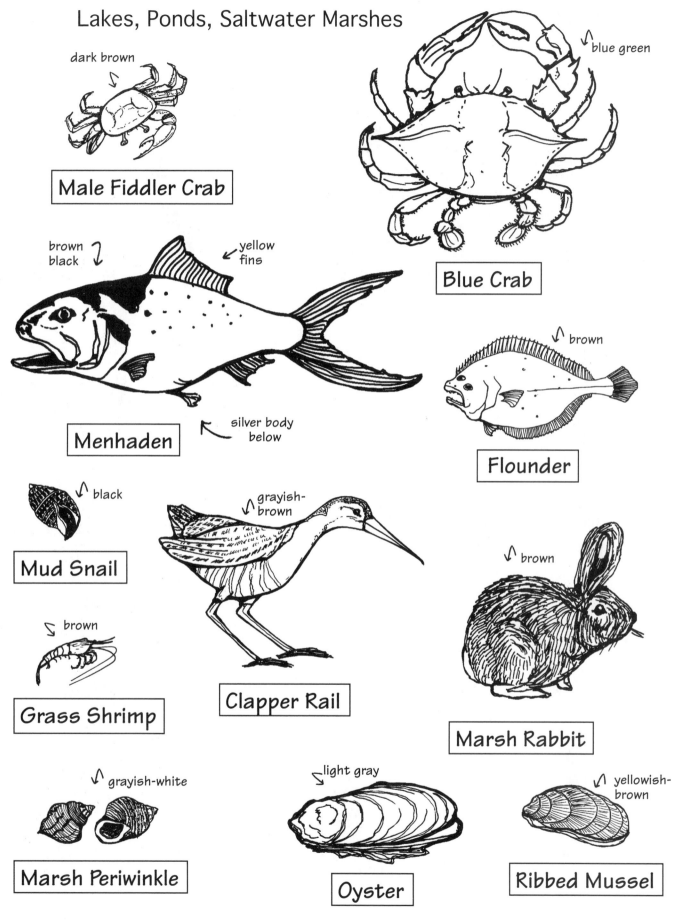

dark brown

Male Fiddler Crab

blue green

Blue Crab

brown black

yellow fins

silver body below

Menhaden

brown

Flounder

black

Mud Snail

grayish-brown

brown

brown

Grass Shrimp

Clapper Rail

Marsh Rabbit

grayish-white

light gray

yellowish-brown

Marsh Periwinkle

Oyster

Ribbed Mussel

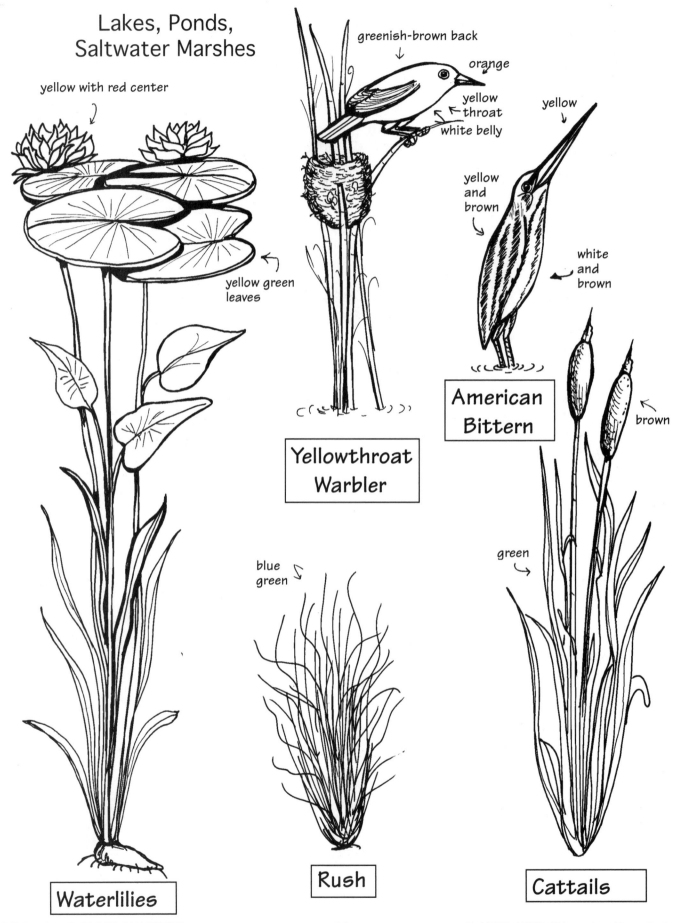

Lakes, Ponds, Saltwater Marshes

yellow with red center

greenish-brown back

orange

yellow throat

white belly

yellow green leaves

yellow

yellow and brown

white and brown

American Bittern

brown

Yellowthroat Warbler

blue green

green

Waterlilies

Rush

Cattails

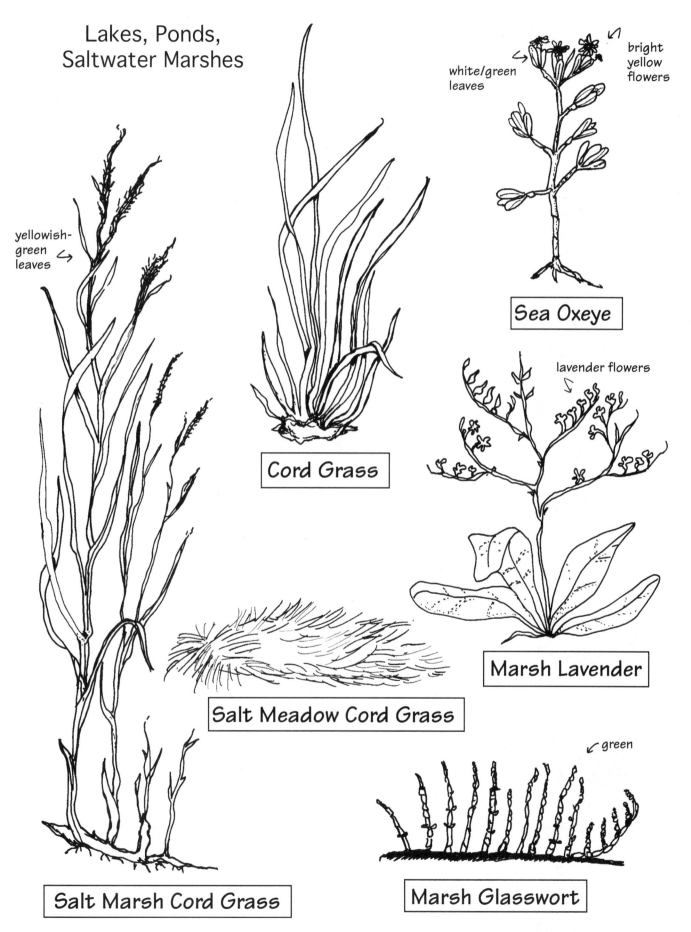

Lakes, Ponds,
Saltwater Marshes

white/green
leaves

bright
yellow
flowers

Sea Oxeye

yellowish-
green
leaves

lavender flowers

Cord Grass

Marsh Lavender

green

Salt Meadow Cord Grass

Salt Marsh Cord Grass

Marsh Glasswort

Lakes, Ponds, and Saltwater Marshes

Leopard Frog   **(Amphibian)**

This is the frog most frequently hunted for its legs. The leopard frog moves around and hunts mostly at night. It is 5-13 cm (2-5 in) long with powerful hind legs. Its green color with dark green spots helps it to hide in the weeds along the banks of lakes and ponds to escape its predators. It lives on insects, spiders, small fish, and anything else that can be caught and swallowed. The leopard frog lays masses of **frog eggs** numbering up to 20,000 in shallow water. These eggs hatch within a month becoming **tadpoles**. The brownish tadpoles spend their time in the water eating water plants and algae and in six to 24 months become frogs.

Spotted Newt   **(Amphibian)**

Newts are small salamanders that live in or near the water. They average 7-13 cm (3-5 in) in length. Newts can often be found foraging in shallow water for worms, insects, frogs eggs, and larvae. The newts' eggs hatch in water and later are transformed into red land-dwelling creatures called efts. In one to three years efts become adults with olive green bodies with red spots. They then return to the water.

Spotted Salamander   **(Amphibian)**

A salamander looks much like a lizard, but its skin is thin and moist. The spotted salamander can be found in the woods and hillsides near water. It spends much of its time underground, where it is damp and it has few enemies. It has a stout black body with rows of yellow spots down its back. It is 13-24 cm (5-9 in) in length. The female lays one or more compact, clear egg masses, each containing about 100 eggs. This amphibian may live 20 years.

Oyster   **(Mollusk)**

Oysters are often located in clusters attached to each other in the saltwater marshes. Large numbers of these clusters are called an oyster bed. Only one of the two shells of an oyster can move. Inside it is a fleshy tan-gray blob. An oyster is different from a clam in that it has no developed foot for movement. It also has no siphon and only one muscle to open its shell. Oysters open their shells and filter water during the time of high tide. They are 5-20 cm (2-8 in) long.

Marsh Periwinkles   **(Mollusk)**

Marsh periwinkles are acorn-sized snails seen crawling on salt grass where they eat algae and decaying plants. Periwinkles move up and down the cord grass in response to the tides, high when the tide is in and low when the tide is out. Their shells are spiral in shape. They are gray white in color with an orange streak on one side of the shell opening. Periwinkles are edible.

Lakes, Ponds, and Saltwater Marshes

	Mud Snail (Mollusk) The mud snail is found in great numbers on tidal mud flats and in the marsh areas. It is found in dense clusters of hundreds in the muddy marshes. This hardy snail's shell is small and colored a dull black. It feeds on dead animals.
	Ribbed Mussel (Mollusk) The ribbed mussel lives in the salt marsh. It attaches itself among the roots of the marsh grass. The mussel lies buried except for a small portion at its wide end, which sticks above the mud. The mussel opens its shell at high tide and feeds by straining plankton, bacteria, and organic detritus from the water. The mussel has a rough yellowish-brown shell 10 cm (4 in) long.
	Blue Crab (Crustacean) The blue crab has five pairs of legs. The first pair of legs is modified pincers. The next three are walking legs, while the last pair is modified into paddle-like structures for swimming. The blue crab has eyes at the end of moveable stalks. These stalks give the blue crab the ability to see 360 degrees as well as the ability to retract the eyes into grooves on its shell when danger threatens. If the blue crab loses a leg in a battle, it is able to grow another one. It can crawl across the bottom of the marsh, swim rapidly, or even burrow into the sandy bottom for protection. It eats dead animals. The blue crab is 23 cm (9 in) wide and 10 cm (4 in) long, blue green on top and white on the bottom.
	Fiddler Crab (Crustacean) Groups of dark brown fiddler crabs can be seen congregating and scurrying around the marsh at low tide. The male fiddler can be easily distinguished from the female. The male has an oversized claw on one side, which it uses to defend territory and attract a mate. The burrow of the fiddler crab is easy to spot. It is a dime-sized hole with stacks of soil pellets beside it. The fiddler crab uses its burrow for protection from predators and from the daily flooding of high tide. When the tide comes in, the fiddler places a mud plug in its burrow, keeping it dry until the tide recedes. It feeds on organic matter. The fiddler is a small, 2.5 cm (1 in), fast-moving crab.
	Grass Shrimp (Crustacean) The grass shrimp has a segmented body, jointed legs, stalked eyes, and hard external skeleton. It has 19 sets of paired appendages, including antennae for feeling, jaws for eating, legs for walking, and swimmerets for swimming. It spawns in the ocean, but the immature stages develop in the estuaries. The adult shrimp is a scavenger feeding on a variety of plants and animals in the salt marsh.
	Small Fry Fish (Fish) These are numerous small silver fish that feed on insects, weeds, and algae scraped from the rocks. They average in length from 2-8 cm (1-3 in). Small fry fish are food for numerous birds, mammals, and larger fish.

Lakes, Ponds, and Saltwater Marshes

	Snapping Turtle (Reptile) 　　The snapping turtle is one of the largest turtles living in fresh water. It is 20-44 cm (8-18 in) in length. It has a large head with powerful hooked jaws, long tail, and relatively small brown shell. It lives in quiet mud-bottomed ponds and lakes. The snapping turtle eats a wide variety of aquatic plants and animals. It can usually be seen floating just below the pond's surface. It is an excellent swimmer. A snapper can inflict a serious bite on any hand that lifts it from the water or teases it. The female lays 25-50 eggs which hatch in two to three months. The baby snappers make their way to the water where they will spend their first few years. Snapping turtles can live up to 60 years.
	Painted Turtle (Reptile) 　　The painted turtle can often be found sunning itself on a log with dozens of other turtles. It likes to live in a shallow pond or lake with weeds and half-submerged logs. This green turtle with red and yellow markings is 10-24 cm (4-10 in) long with a smooth shell. The young turtle eats snails, crayfish, and tadpoles, but the adult turtle eats only water plants.
	Green Water Snake (Reptile) 　　The green water snake prefers to live in a swamp area that has trees around it so it can bask in the branches that overhang the water. It is a heavy-bodied, green-colored snake, 60-120 cm (2-4 ft) long. It feeds on minnows and small fish. It is not a venomous snake, but it can inflict a painful bite when it is captured. An especially adept swimmer and diver, it will slither through the water to capture its prey. The female snake will give birth to 4-100 live young.
	Yellow Perch (Fish) 　　The yellow perch is a valued sport fish that is found in clear water of lakes and streams. It is a slender-bodied fish that can grow to a length of 30 cm (12 in) and weigh 500 g (1 lb). It is yellow in color with orange yellow fins. The perch feeds on small fish and crustaceans.
	Bluegill (Fish) 　　The bluegill is a deep-bodied, flat-sided fish. It has a red orange colored body with yellow green fins and a blue green color on top. It usually can be found in quiet, weedy ponds and mud-bottomed streams. It usually feeds on insects. The bluegill is 20-30 cm (8-12 in) in length.
	Catfish (Fish) 　　This is a fish that locates its food by probing the bottom with its sensitive whiskers. The catfish is important to commercial and sport fishermen. It spends time near the bottom of lakes and rivers. It feeds on other fish and aquatic insects. The catfish is 5-100 cm (2-40 in) in length.

Lakes, Ponds, and Saltwater Marshes

	Stickleback **(Fish)** The stickleback is a slender green fish named for the row of spines along its back. It is found in small lakes and shallow ponds. It eats crustaceans, insects, and algae. The male stickleback makes an intricate, suspended nest of plant stems. After the female stickleback lays her eggs, the male guards the eggs and young. The stickleback is 5-8 cm (2-3 in) in length.
	Menhaden **(Fish)** The menhaden is a member of the herring family. The adult fish is a filter feeder that inhabits the salt marsh. It is brown on top, silver below, and its fins are yellow. A menhaden's mouth is large. It has a distinct black spot behind its head. It is an essential link in many ocean food chains. It is 46 cm (18 in) long.
	Flounder **(Fish)** The flounder is a flat fish. Its body is flattened into an oval pancake shape, 18 cm (7 in) long. The underside of a flounder is white with its top being a brownish color with darker spots and colors. The camouflage nature protects it from predators and lets it sneak up on small fish and shrimp. The flounder is sideways oriented; it actually lies and swims on its side. It is found in saltwater marshes.
	Great Diving Beetle **(Insect)** The great diving beetle is a fierce hunter and its larva has earned the title of "watertiger." This brown black beetle, which is from 2-7 cm (1-3 in) long, is oval in shape. It has front legs that act like claws to grasp its food. It feeds on insects and other small creatures. The beetle is a strong swimmer using its back legs to push itself through the water. It carries a supply of air under each wing which is taken into the body through rows of holes under the wing cases. The female lays her eggs in the spring inside the stems of plants growing in the water. The eggs hatch into brown **larvae** which feed in the pond, then in about a year they dig into the mud at the edge of the pond and change into pupae. In three weeks, the pupae becomes adult beetles and return to the pond.
	Dragonfly **(Insect)** This beautiful, graceful creature is able to hover, fly backward and forward, and make abrupt turns like a helicopter. It has a long slender body that is usually brown or black. The wings are transparent and are held straight out from the body when the dragonfly is at rest. The dragonfly measures 5-10 cm (2-4 in) in length, however its wing span is longer than its body. This insect can be found most often near streams, lakes, and ponds. A fierce predator, it destroys huge numbers of mosquitoes. It lays its eggs on water plants or just under the surface of the water, and the eggs hatch into **dragonfly nymphs** which live underwater for several years. The golden brown nymphs are aggressive hunters living on water insects and small fish. Eventually, the nymphs become adult dragonflies and leave the water to fly in the air.

Lakes, Ponds, and Saltwater Marshes

	Mosquito (Insect) This is probably one of the most unpopular flying creatures known to humans. This small insect is less than 1 cm (0.33 in) in length and is found worldwide. The mosquito cannot eat solid food, it can only take in liquids. It sucks the liquids through its needlelike mouth parts like a straw. Only the female mosquito feeds on blood; the male lives on plant juices and nectar. The blood the female drinks provides her eggs with important nutrients. She lays her eggs in standing water where they hatch into larvae. After going through the pupa stage they become adult mosquitoes. Efforts have been made to eliminate the mosquito through draining wetlands and using insecticides, but these methods have proved ineffective.
	Water Striders (Insect) If you see a long thin bug skating along the still surface of a pond or lake, it is most likely a water strider. It uses the "skin" formed by the surface tension on water to support its weight. The water strider lives on larvae and insects that live or fall on the surface of the water. It is a small insect, about 2 cm (0.75 in) long, with a dark blue or brown coloration.
	Mayfly (Insect) The mayfly's name comes from the fact that the adult stage of the insect comes out of the water in May. Young mayflies (nymphs) live underwater and feed on plants. The winged adult stage lives only for a short time and eats nothing; its main purpose is to reproduce. The fragile looking insect is 3 cm (1.25 in) long. Its triangular-shaped wings are transparent and held vertical to its body. The body is mainly speckled brown or yellow color.
	Water Scorpion (Insect) The water scorpion is a golden-brown, stick-like bug with front legs that resemble claws. Its other legs are long and thin. It has thread-like breathing tubes that extend from the back of its body. The water scorpion lives in ponds and lakes where it preys on other insects, tadpoles, and small fish. It is 3-5 cm (1-2 in) long with 2.1 cm (1 in) breathing tubes.
	Beaver (Mammal) The beaver is one animal that can drastically change its habitat to suit its needs. It is found near lakes and streams where it cuts down trees to build its own dam and create a pond. This golden-brown animal was hunted extensively for its fur to make hats and coats. It is 90-120 cm (3-4 ft) long and weighs 18 to 27 kg (40-60 lbs). It feeds on the bark, twigs, and tubers of trees and plants around the pond. Its 40 cm (16 in) tail resembles a scaly paddle and is used as a rudder and an alarm sounder when it is slapped on the water. The female beaver produces up to eight babies called kits. The beaver has a life span of 15 to 21 years.

Lakes, Ponds, and Saltwater Marshes

Mink   (Mammal)
Clothed in rich brown fur, the mink is equally at home in the water or on the land. A ferocious hunter, the mink eats a great variety of food. Fish, muskrats, snakes, mice, and birds are a few of the items on its menu. Mink measure 70 cm (28 in) long and weigh up to 1.6 kg (3.5 lbs). Large owls, coyotes, and bobcats prey on the mink. Humans also prey on the mink for their soft luxurious fur. Mink live about three years. The female mink can have 2-10 young.

Raccoon   (Mammal)
The raccoon is a small animal which was called "he who scratches with his hands" by the Native American Indians. Its sensitive hands are always busy, scratching, exploring, feeling, and poking around for food. A raccoon measures about 80 cm (32 in), including tail, and usually weighs about 9 kg (20 lbs). The female raccoon will have 1-7 young. This brownish-gray creature with a ringed tail and eye mask, is equally at home in the water as it is on land. It will eat almost any type of food: nuts, berries, bird eggs, rodents, insects, fish, frogs, and crayfish are relished. Raccoons live 10 or more years in the wild.

Marsh Rabbit   (Mammal)
The marsh rabbit looks very similar to the cottontail rabbit. One noticeable difference is that it has shorter ears and a very small tail. These rabbits forage for plants along the edge of the marsh. It has several litters per year with two to five babies each time. It is 35-43 cm (14-18 in) long.

Brown Bat   (Mammal)
The brown bat has dense, glossy brown fur. It is a small animal, averaging 7 to 20 g (0.25-0.75 oz) in weight, 8-13 cm (3-5 in) in length. It lives on flying insects (moths, mosquitoes, beetles, flies), which it finds by sending out high-pitched sounds that bounce off objects and come back as echoes (called echolocation). The brown bat can most often be seen flying at twilight over meadows or suburban streets. During the day it is found hanging upside down in a cave or building. The bat has only one baby a year. It lives up to 18 years.

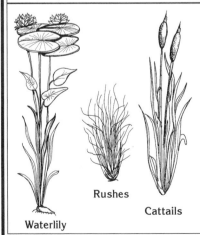

Waterlily
Rushes
Cattails

Pond Plants   (Plants)
In the shallow marshy areas of ponds and ditches, **cattails** can be found. They are very useful plants since the tuber, flowers, and pollen can be used for food and the leaves woven into mats and baskets. It grows 51-220 cm (2-7 ft) tall. Cattails are brown with bright green leaves. They provide an important source of food and shelter for water birds and wildlife. The **waterlily** is a plant that grows rooted to the bottom of a pond or lake. The stout stalk rises to the surface of the water where the bright, floating blossoms and shiny green oval leaf pads float. The white flowers are 5-15 cm (2-6 in) wide and the leaf is 8-50 cm (3-20 in) across. The resilient stems of the **rushes** can be used for mats, hats, and baskets. The blue green stems grow 30-200 cm (1-6 ft) tall. The plants can be found along riverbanks, lakeshores, and marshes.

Lakes, Ponds, and Saltwater Marshes

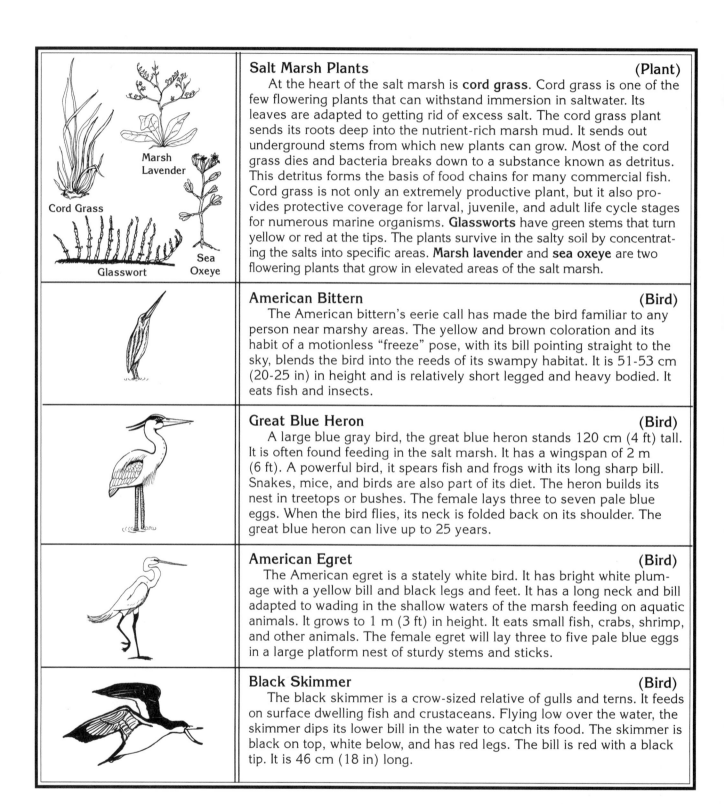

Salt Marsh Plants   (Plant)

At the heart of the salt marsh is **cord grass**. Cord grass is one of the few flowering plants that can withstand immersion in saltwater. Its leaves are adapted to getting rid of excess salt. The cord grass plant sends its roots deep into the nutrient-rich marsh mud. It sends out underground stems from which new plants can grow. Most of the cord grass dies and bacteria breaks down to a substance known as detritus. This detritus forms the basis of food chains for many commercial fish. Cord grass is not only an extremely productive plant, but it also provides protective coverage for larval, juvenile, and adult life cycle stages for numerous marine organisms. **Glassworts** have green stems that turn yellow or red at the tips. The plants survive in the salty soil by concentrating the salts into specific areas. **Marsh lavender** and **sea oxeye** are two flowering plants that grow in elevated areas of the salt marsh.

American Bittern   (Bird)

The American bittern's eerie call has made the bird familiar to any person near marshy areas. The yellow and brown coloration and its habit of a motionless "freeze" pose, with its bill pointing straight to the sky, blends the bird into the reeds of its swampy habitat. It is 51-53 cm (20-25 in) in height and is relatively short legged and heavy bodied. It eats fish and insects.

Great Blue Heron   (Bird)

A large blue gray bird, the great blue heron stands 120 cm (4 ft) tall. It is often found feeding in the salt marsh. It has a wingspan of 2 m (6 ft). A powerful bird, it spears fish and frogs with its long sharp bill. Snakes, mice, and birds are also part of its diet. The heron builds its nest in treetops or bushes. The female lays three to seven pale blue eggs. When the bird flies, its neck is folded back on its shoulder. The great blue heron can live up to 25 years.

American Egret   (Bird)

The American egret is a stately white bird. It has bright white plumage with a yellow bill and black legs and feet. It has a long neck and bill adapted to wading in the shallow waters of the marsh feeding on aquatic animals. It grows to 1 m (3 ft) in height. It eats small fish, crabs, shrimp, and other animals. The female egret will lay three to five pale blue eggs in a large platform nest of sturdy stems and sticks.

Black Skimmer   (Bird)

The black skimmer is a crow-sized relative of gulls and terns. It feeds on surface dwelling fish and crustaceans. Flying low over the water, the skimmer dips its lower bill in the water to catch its food. The skimmer is black on top, white below, and has red legs. The bill is red with a black tip. It is 46 cm (18 in) long.

Lakes, Ponds, and Saltwater Marshes

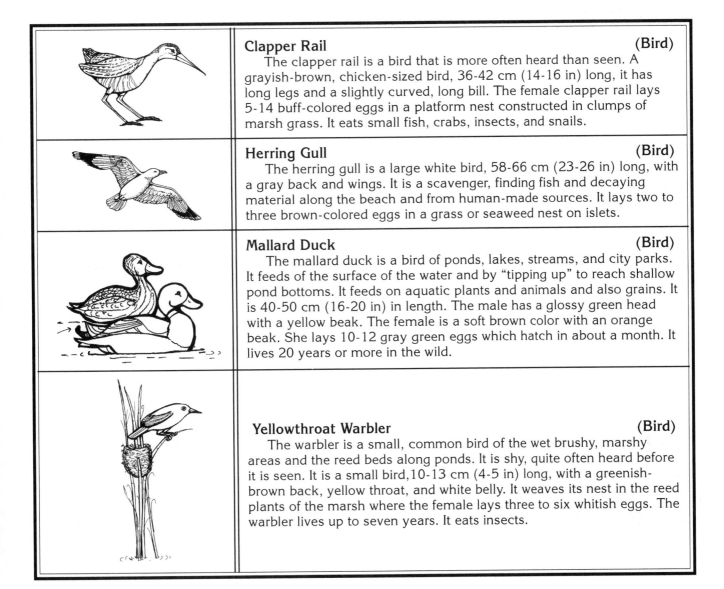

Clapper Rail   (Bird)

The clapper rail is a bird that is more often heard than seen. A grayish-brown, chicken-sized bird, 36-42 cm (14-16 in) long, it has long legs and a slightly curved, long bill. The female clapper rail lays 5-14 buff-colored eggs in a platform nest constructed in clumps of marsh grass. It eats small fish, crabs, insects, and snails.

Herring Gull   (Bird)

The herring gull is a large white bird, 58-66 cm (23-26 in) long, with a gray back and wings. It is a scavenger, finding fish and decaying material along the beach and from human-made sources. It lays two to three brown-colored eggs in a grass or seaweed nest on islets.

Mallard Duck   (Bird)

The mallard duck is a bird of ponds, lakes, streams, and city parks. It feeds of the surface of the water and by "tipping up" to reach shallow pond bottoms. It feeds on aquatic plants and animals and also grains. It is 40-50 cm (16-20 in) in length. The male has a glossy green head with a yellow beak. The female is a soft brown color with an orange beak. She lays 10-12 gray green eggs which hatch in about a month. It lives 20 years or more in the wild.

Yellowthroat Warbler   (Bird)

The warbler is a small, common bird of the wet brushy, marshy areas and the reed beds along ponds. It is shy, quite often heard before it is seen. It is a small bird, 10-13 cm (4-5 in) long, with a greenish-brown back, yellow throat, and white belly. It weaves its nest in the reed plants of the marsh where the female lays three to six whitish eggs. The warbler lives up to seven years. It eats insects.

Living Things of the Lakes, Ponds, and Saltwater Marshes

Living Things	Home	Food	Characteristics
Amphibians			
Leopard Frog	Edge of ponds, lakes, and wetlands	Insects, worms, larvae	Large head, eyes; strong hind legs; long sticky tongue; 5-13 cm (2-5 in)
Frog Eggs	In lakes and ponds		Eggs laid in masses in the shallows; hatch into tadpoles
Tadpoles	In lakes and ponds	Plants, algae	Breathe through gills; live in the water
Spotted Newt	In lakes and ponds	Insects, larvae	Rough skin; lay eggs on water plants; larvae called efts; form and color changes when breeding; 7-13 cm (3-5 in)
Spotted Salamander	In ponds, under stones or rotten logs	Grubs, slugs, insects, worms	Stout body; moist skin; dark brown to black with orange and yellow spots; 13-24 cm (5-9 in)
Reptiles			
Painted Turtle	Shallow, weedy waters	Mollusks, aquatic plants, small animals	Freshwater turtle; bask in sun on logs; smooth, flattened shell; hibernate in muddy bottom; 10-24 cm (4-10 in)
Snapping Turtle	Mud-bottomed waters	Small animals, plants, insects	Big head; long tail; powerful jaws used for protection; float on surface of ponds; good swimmer; 20-44 cm (8-18 in)
Green Water Snake	Tidal marshes, quiet water	Insects, tadpoles, fish, frogs	Live in debris along water; good swimmer; bask in trees and shrubs; non-poisonous; 20-44 cm (8-18 in)
Fish			
Yellow Perch	Clear streams and lakes	Small fish, crustaceans	Valued sport fish; 500 g (1 lb); 30 cm (12 in)
Bluegill	Weedy ponds, mud-bottomed streams	Insects, small animals, crustaceans	Sharp spines on back; flat-sided, deep-bodied; males make nest and protect eggs; 20-30 cm (8-12 in)

Living Things of the Lakes, Ponds, and Saltwater Marshes

Living Things	Home	Food	Characteristics
Catfish	Streams and rivers	Small fish and animals	Locate food by barbels (sensory organ) around mouth; a sport fish; spend time at bottom of lake; no scales; 5-100 cm (2-40 in)
Stickleback	Cool, shallow water	Insects, small fish	Small fish with stout dorsal spikes; elongated body; build nest of sticks and roots; 5-8 cm (2-3 in)
Menhaden	Salt marsh, estuaries	Plankton	Filter feeder; brown on top, silver below; 46 cm (18 in)
Flounder	Shallow water over sand; salt marsh	Fish, shrimp	Flat fish; sideways oriented; white on bottom, brown on top; 18 cm (7 in)
Insects			
Dragonfly	Near freshwater	Mosquitoes, insects	Long, slender body; transparent wings; fast flier; large compound eyes; can fly forward and backward; 5-10 cm (2-4 in)
Dragonfly Nymph	In freshwater	Insect larvae, tadpoles, fish	Thick body; big head and mouth; crawl on bottom; remain in water 1-5 years; eat anything they catch; eaten by larger fish; 2.5 cm (1 in)
Mayfly	Fields, forest	Adult stage does not eat insects	Fragile; three long "tails"; triangular wings; huge swarms in spring; larvae called nymphs; eaten by fish; 1.5-3 cm (0.60-1.25 in)
Water Strider	Ponds, lakes	Small animals	Slender body; long legs; skate about on surface of water; 2 cm (0.75 in)
Water Scorpion	Ponds, lakes	Blood, plant juices, nectar, insects, small animals	Stick-like; two breathing tubes at end of abdomen; front legs catch tadpoles and small fish; 3-5 cm (1-2 in)

Living Things of the Lakes, Ponds, and Saltwater Marshes

Living Things	Home	Food	Characteristics
Mosquito	On land near water	Bark, twigs, water plants	Long legs; soft body; female has piercing mouthpiece; bite can spread disease; eggs float on water; less than 1 cm (0.33 in)
Great Diving Beetle	In ponds and lakes	Fish, muskrats, snakes	Long, strong swimmer; larva called "water tiger"; fierce hunter; 2-7 cm (1-3 in)
Mammals			
Beaver	Near lakes and streams	Mice, birds	Long golden brown fur; build dams to create ponds; 90-120 cm (3-4 ft)
Mink	On water or on land	Nuts, berries, bird eggs	Rich brown fur which is desired by humans; 70 cm (28 in)
Raccoon	On land	Fish, crayfish	Brownish-gray; ringed tail; eye mask; 80 cm (32 in)
Marsh Rabbit	Marshy areas	Grasses	Dark brown body; small tail; short ears; 35-43 cm (14-18 in)
Brown Bat	Cave or building	Moth, mosquitoes, beetles, flies	Glossy brown fur; 7-20 g (0.25-0.75 oz); 8-13 cm (3-5 in)
Mollusks			
Oyster	Estuaries	Plankton	Grayish; common edible oyster; 5-20 cm (2-8 in)
Marsh Periwinkle	Marshy area	Algae, decaying plants	Acorn-sized snail; gray white spiral-shape shell
Mud Snail	Mud flats	Dead marine animals	Small black snail found in great numbers
Ribbed Mussel	Salt marsh	Plankton, bacteria	Yellowish-brown shell; attaches to a solid object; 10 cm (4 in)

Living Things of the Lakes, Ponds, and Saltwater Marshes

Living Things	Home	Food	Characteristics
Crustaceans			
Blue Crab	Estuaries	Dead animals	Blue green on top; white on bottom; common edible crab; 23 cm (9 in) wide; 10 cm (4 in) long
Fiddler Crab	Marshy area	Organic matter	Dark, little crab; male has one large and one small claw; female has two small claws; 25 mm (1 in)
Grass Shrimp	Salt marsh	Plants, animals	Brown color; segmented bodies, jointed legs; stalked eyes; 17 cm (7 in)
Birds			
American Bittern	Marshy area	Fish, small crustaceans, insects	Yellow and brown color; stand with bill pointing straight up; 51-53 cm (20-25 in)
Great Blue Heron	Marshy area, ponds	Fish, frogs, snakes, mice	Large blue gray bird; flies with neck folded back on shoulder; 120 cm (4 ft) tall; wingspan 2 m (6 ft)
Mallard Duck	Ponds, lakes	Plants, animals	Common bird in city parks; male has glossy green head; female has soft brown feathers; 40-50 cm (16-20 in)
Yellowthroat Warbler	Marshy, wet areas	Insects	Greenish-brown back; yellow throat; white belly; 10-13 cm (4-5 in)
Black Skimmer	Marshy areas	Fish, crustaceans	Black below; white above; flattened bill with the lower part longer than the upper part; 46 cm (18 in)
Clapper Rail	Marshy areas	Insects, crabs, fish, snails	More commonly heard than seen; grayish-brown; long legs; long bill; 36-42 cm (14-16 in)
Herring Gull	Coastal areas	Fish, decaying refuse	White; light gray back and wings; 58-66 cm (23-26 in)
American Egret	Wetlands	Small fish, shrimp, crabs	White bird with black legs and feet; yellow bill; 1 m (3 ft) tall

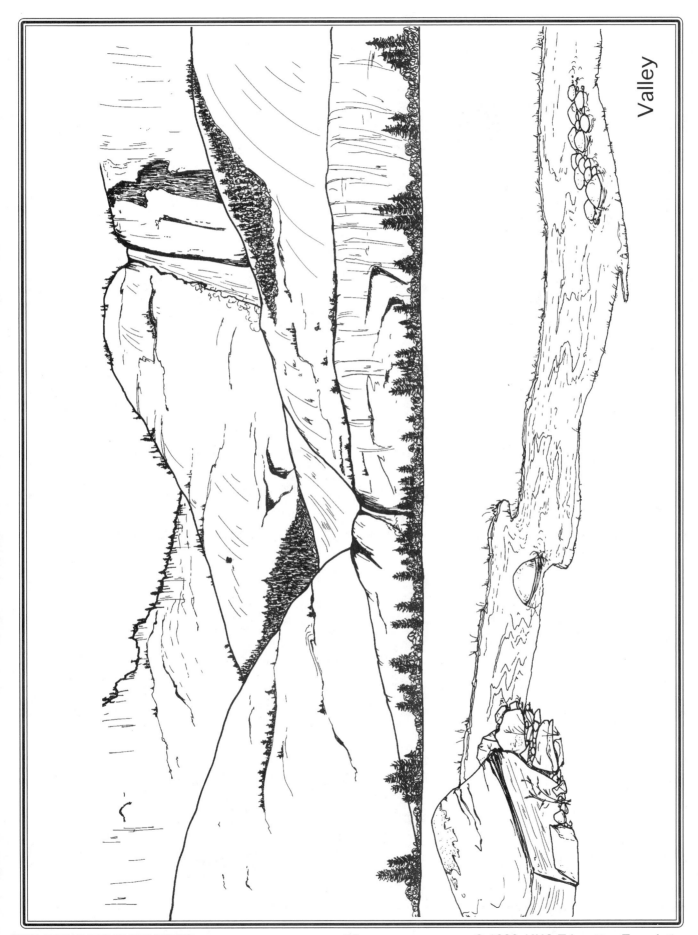

Valley

Valley

Flowing rivers, grinding glaciers, and the sinking of the Earth's surface have all played a role in creating natural depressions in the Earth's surface. These depressions can be called gorges, canyons, basins, or valleys.

Valleys can be caused by streams that begin in the higher elevations and cut into the land as they flow downhill. Almost all valleys formed by running water start out V-shaped. Young valleys have narrow floors. (The bottom of the valley is called the floor.) In middle-age or old-age valleys, the floor is wider, sometimes many miles across.

A valley can be formed by the erosion of a glacier which has plowed its way down from the highlands. The resulting valley is often in a U-shape. The ice has scraped the walls of the valley and cut deeply into the floor depositing the soil, rocks, and other debris in front of, to the side of, or underneath the glacier.

A valley can also be shaped by the uplifting or sinking of the Earth's surface. These changes in elevation are then influenced by water and wind erosion that widens the depressions, producing a valley.

Valleys vary in size, use, elevation, and appearance. For example, the broad flat Central Valley of California and the lush Shenandoah Valley of Virginia both have rich farmlands. The magnificent Yosemite Valley with its high granite walls and U-shape attracts visitors from around the world. The stark, desolate, but beautiful Death Valley is the lowest spot in the United States. The heavily populated Hudson River Valley has attracted people to settle along the banks of the river from early pioneer days. The Rio Grande River Valley separates the United States from Mexico and its waters provide sustenance for many crops grown along it.

People are attracted to the flat land on the floor of the valleys. There they can construct their towns and build industries, highways, and railroads. After numerous years of rivers depositing silt, many valley soils are very fertile. This is good farming land for their crops and grazing land for their animals.

76

Many wild birds and animals live in the valleys close to humans. The smaller animals such as opossums, raccoons, squirrels, skunks, rabbits, and pocket gophers fill a very important niche in the food chain of the valleys. The carnivorous birds, barn owls and red-tailed hawks, are numerous wherever they can find their favorite

food, rodents and other small mammals. The flicker, quail, killdeer, mourning dove, and meadowlark are residents where grains are present for them to eat.

Larger animal are present in outlying areas away from the human residents. Mule deer, bobcats, coyotes, foxes, and badgers are some of the important animal residents that find food and shelter in the valleys.

Valleys have always been the corridors in our nation's history, they provided natural passageways to explorers and settlers.

Valley

bright blue blossoms
with yellow centers

green stems
and leaves

Blue-Eyed Grasses

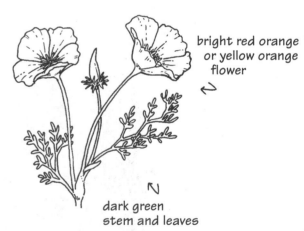

bright red orange
or yellow orange
flower

dark green
stem and leaves

California Poppy

Science Buddy

78

Valley

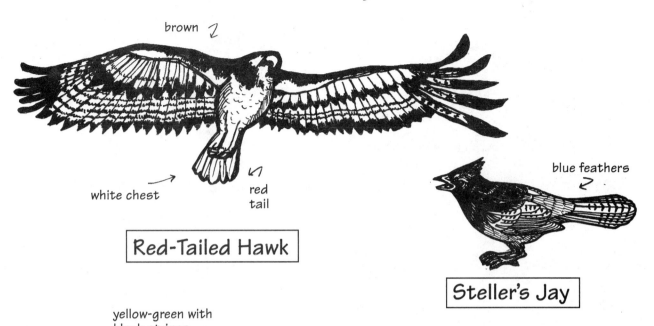

brown

white chest

red tail

Red-Tailed Hawk

blue feathers

Steller's Jay

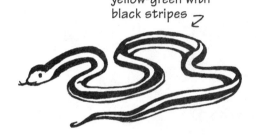

yellow-green with black stripes

Garter Snake

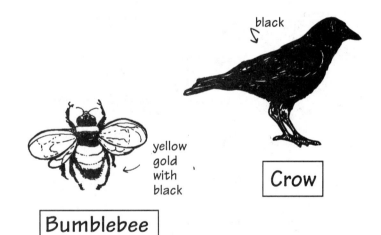

yellow gold with black

black

Crow

Bumblebee

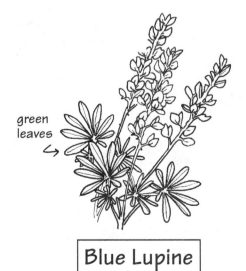

green leaves

Blue Lupine

reddish-brown sides

white stripe

grayish back

white belly

Chipmunk

79

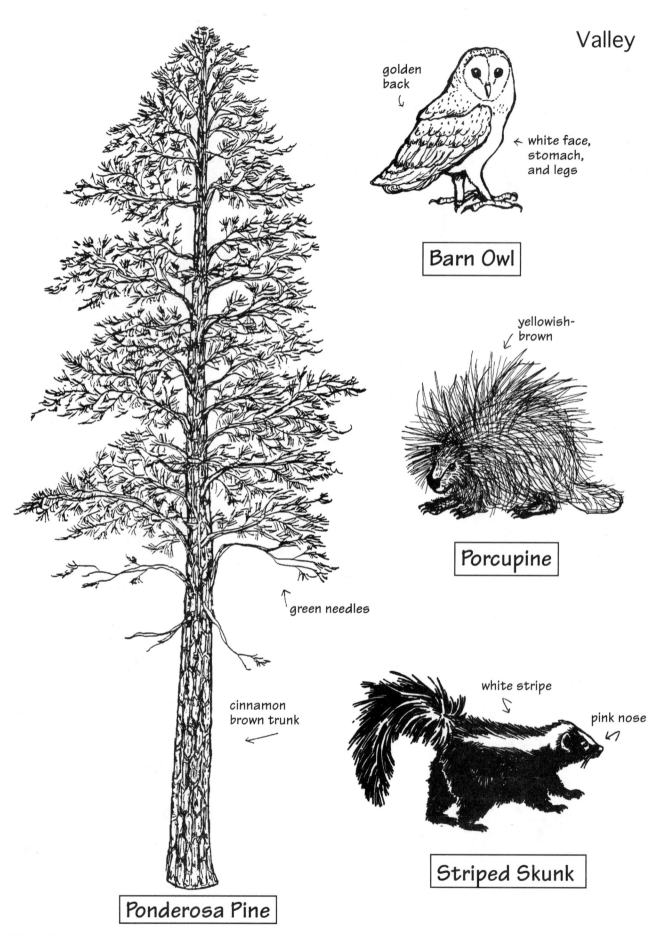

Valley

golden
back

white face,
stomach,
and legs

Barn Owl

yellowish-
brown

Porcupine

green needles

cinnamon
brown trunk

white stripe

pink nose

Striped Skunk

Ponderosa Pine

Valley

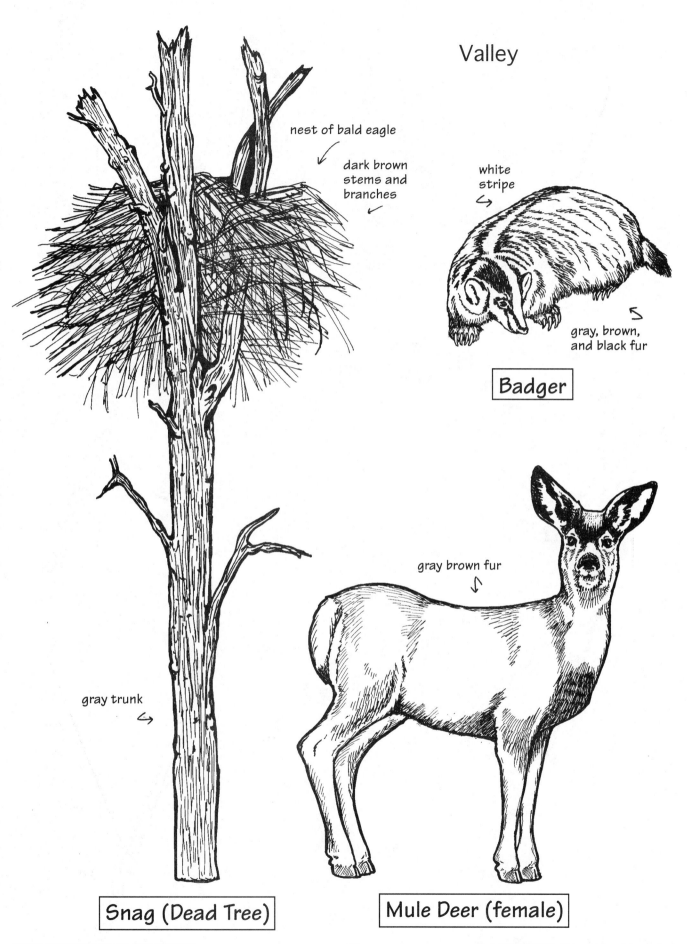

nest of bald eagle

dark brown stems and branches

white stripe

gray, brown, and black fur

Badger

gray brown fur

gray trunk

Snag (Dead Tree)

Mule Deer (female)

81

Valley

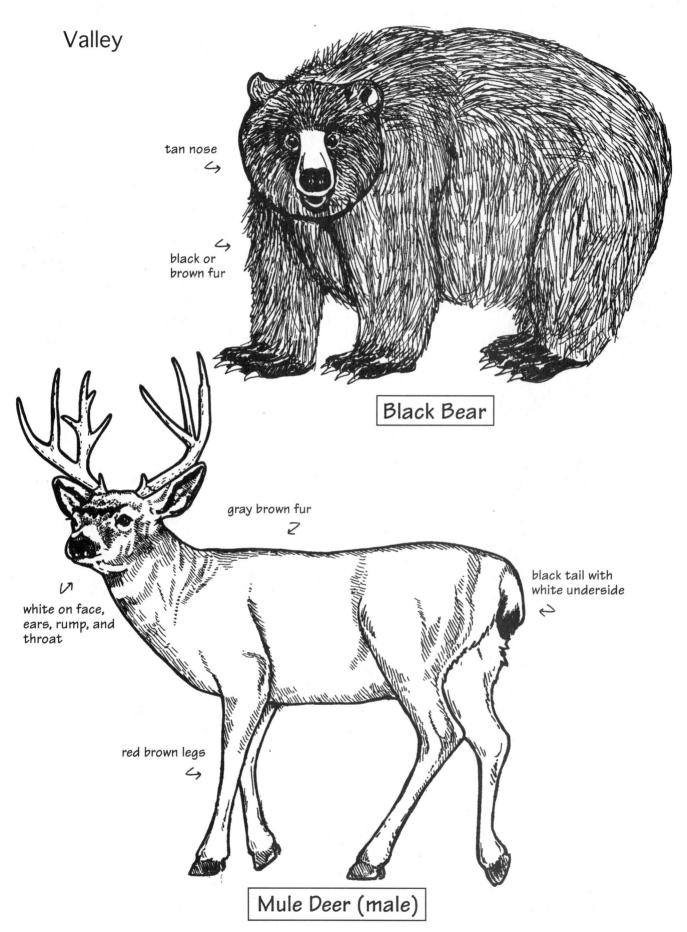

tan nose

black or
brown fur

Black Bear

gray brown fur

black tail with
white underside

white on face,
ears, rump, and
throat

red brown legs

Mule Deer (male)

Valley

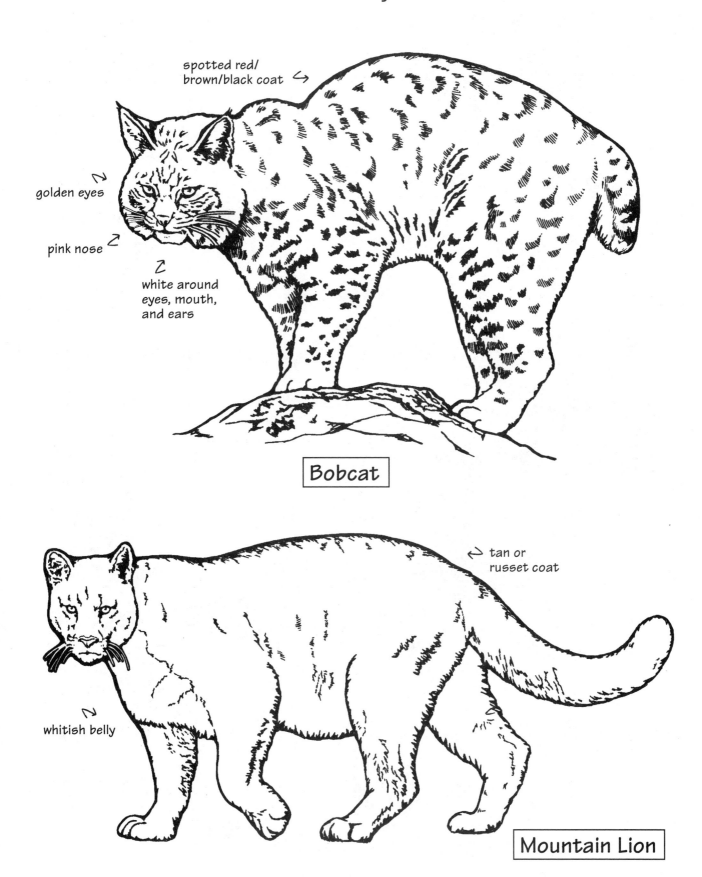

spotted red/
brown/black coat

golden eyes

pink nose

white around
eyes, mouth,
and ears

Bobcat

tan or
russet coat

whitish belly

Mountain Lion

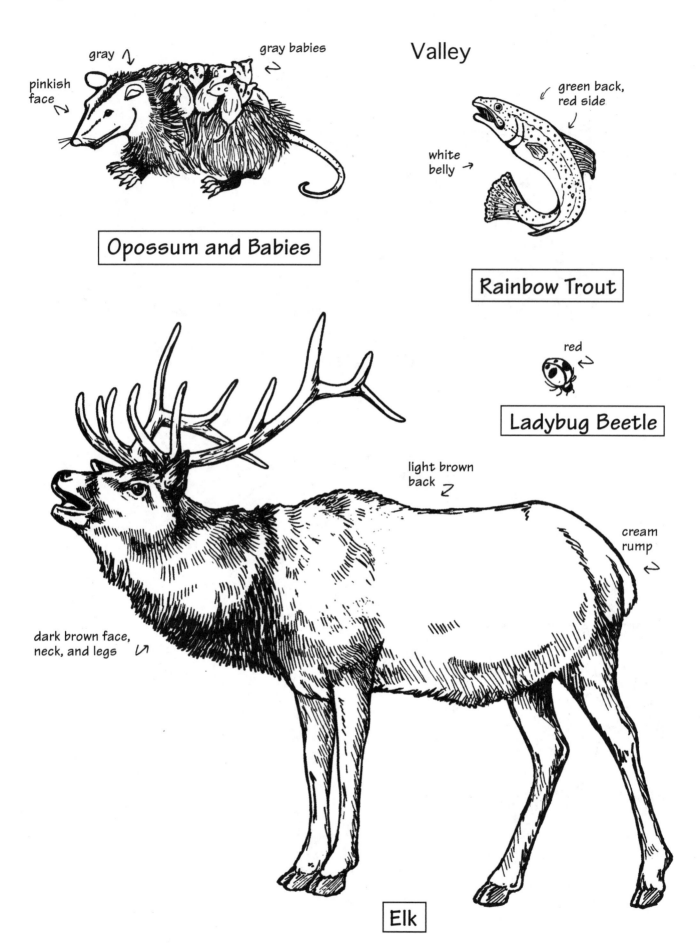

gray

gray babies

Valley

pinkish face

Opossum and Babies

green back, red side

white belly

Rainbow Trout

red

Ladybug Beetle

light brown back

cream rump

dark brown face, neck, and legs

Elk

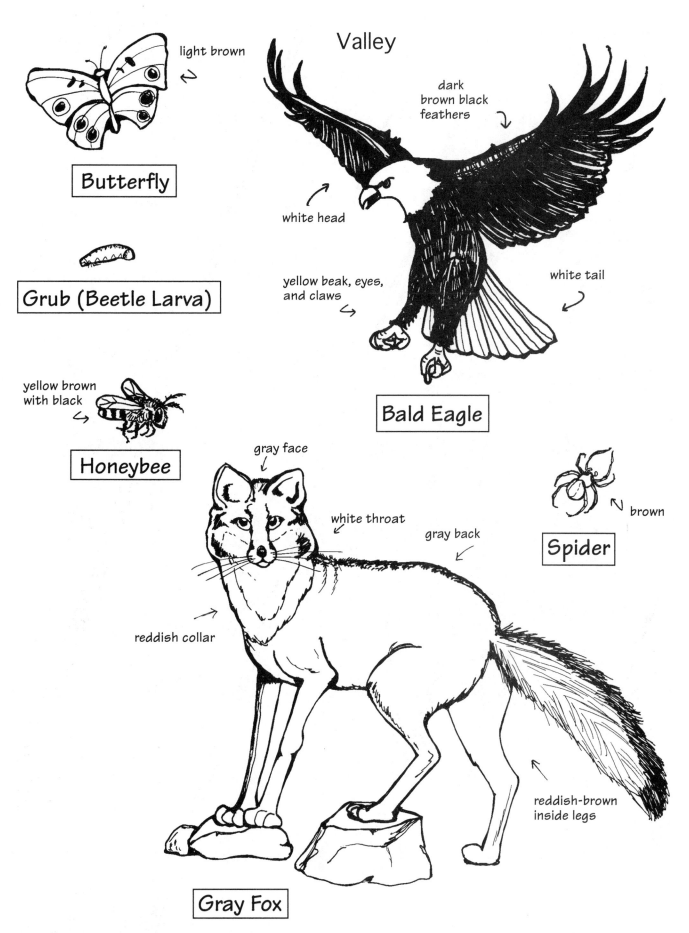

Butterfly

light brown

Valley

dark brown black feathers

white head

yellow beak, eyes, and claws

white tail

Bald Eagle

Grub (Beetle Larva)

yellow brown with black

Honeybee

gray face

white throat

gray back

Spider

brown

reddish collar

reddish-brown inside legs

Gray Fox

leaves green in summer,
yellow gold in fall

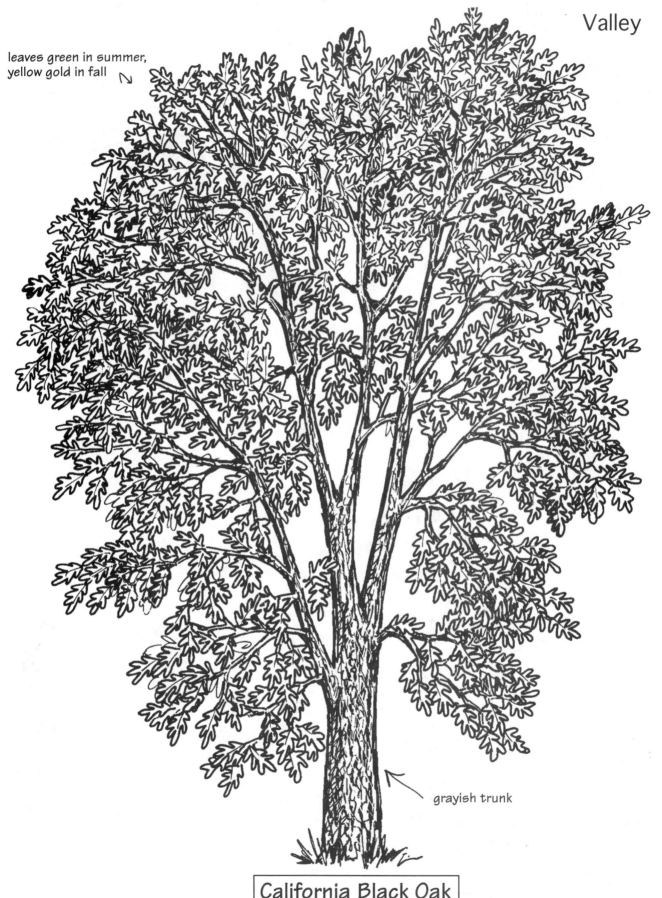

grayish trunk

California Black Oak

86

Living Things of the Valley

Black Bear (Mammal)

The black bear is a powerful, thick-furred animal with small, rounded ears and small eyes which are set close together. Its vision is poor, but its sense of smell is keen. It spends much of its active life looking for food. Although classified as a carnivore, the black bear tends to be omnivorous, eating leaves, berries, fruit, and insects; only occasionally will it hunt small mammals and fish. In the autumn, the bear gains weight and retreats into a den in a cave, under a fallen tree, or in a hollow tree to sleep for several months, living off its stored fat. It is in this den that the female black bear gives birth every two years to two or three cubs. The black bear has a lifespan of about 25 years. It is 1.2-1.8 m (4-6 ft) in length and weighs 95-230 kg (200-500 lb). While the black bear may appear clumsy because of its size and shuffling walk, it can climb trees and run quickly. The black bear can be black, but it can also have a rusty brown or gray coat.

Bobcat (Mammal)

The bobcat is a tawny-colored cat with black spots, tufted ears, and a bobbed tail. It roams the mountain and valley areas. Named for its stumpy tail, the bobcat is 60-110 cm (25-42 in) long and weighs 6-12 kg (13-25 lb). It aggressively hunts at night for rabbits, squirrels, and any other small mammals that it can catch. The bobcat is the most common of the small wild cats, but it is so secretive it is rarely seen. The female bobcat usually has three kittens that are born in a cozy den in a rocky area of the mountains.

Badger (Mammal)

The badger has very strong front feet for digging. When threatened it will dig its way out of sight. This gray creature with black and white markings has a flattened body, short legs, and shaggy fur. The badger is a true omnivore; it eats plants, worms, insects, moles, and rats. The badger's only natural enemies are humans who want its fine hair for artist and shaving brushes. The female badger has a litter of one to five young in the spring. The badger is about 44-60 cm (18-22 in) in length and weighs between 9-17 kg (20-36 lb).

Chipmunk (Mammal)

The little reddish-brown animal that you see scurrying over the ground and occasionally up a tree could be a chipmunk. It makes a nest underground, beneath rocks, in fallen trees, or in a burrow. In the nest the female chipmunk will bear a litter of four to five young. It is a very inquisitive creature and can often be seen chattering at an intruder from the limb of a tree. The chipmunk forages on the ground where it collects nuts, seeds, and berries which it stuffs into its cheek pockets to carry to its burrow. There it hides the loot to eat during the winter months when it wakes from its sleep. The chipmunk will also eat slugs, insects, and caterpillars. A chipmunk is about 9-11 cm (3.5-4.5 in) long with a tail that is just about as long. It has a small, slim body with dark and light stripes on its head, sides, and back. The chipmunk lives for about two to three years.

Living Things of the Valley

Elk   (Mammal)

The elk is a large brown animal with a thick neck, slender legs, and a large rack of antlers. It has a dark brown neck and a light rump patch. The elk feeds mainly on grasses and plants. It is 2.4-3 m (7.5-9.5 ft) long and stands 125-150 cm (4-5 ft) tall at the shoulder and weighs as much as 500 kg (1100 lb). The elk's main predator is the mountain lion. The elk is widely distributed in the mountains, forests, and valleys of the western United States. The female gives birth to one or two young.

Gray Fox   (Mammal)

A very shy creature, the gray fox lives near humans but is rarely seen. It spends its days hiding in tree hollows or among the rocks, then it comes out at night to hunt. The gray fox's diet consists of fruit and vegetation, but it will also consume mice, birds, and eggs. It is one of the few foxes that is able to climb trees. The fox has a long bushy tail, 10-30 cm (4-12 in) long, that helps it balance itself in the trees. Its body is about 60-75 cm (2-2.5 ft) long. It has a grayish coat with a band of reddish fur around the neck, legs, feet, and tail. The female will have three to four cubs in a well-hidden den. It can live for about six years.

Porcupine   (Mammal)

A slow shuffling animal with short ears and button eyes, the porcupine looks like an easy dinner. But this prickly animal has 30,000 barbed quills to discourage anything that wants to fool with it. It is the only mammal in North America with sharp spines on its back and tail. The porcupine can most often be found in the top of a tree where it is feasting on its favorite foods — the buds, leaves, twigs, and inner bark of the tree. A yellowish-brown, chunky animal, it is 46-65 cm (18-26 in) in length. The porcupine does not throw its quills, but imbeds them in any unlucky victim by swatting them with its tail. The female porcupine has a single baby that can climb a tree within a week of its birth. It can live 10 years or more. The porcupine has very few predators, one of these being the mountain lion.

Striped Skunk   (Mammal)

The small black and white striped creature waddling along in the woods at dusk is probably a striped skunk. It is hunting for grasshoppers, beetles, crickets, beetle grubs, and earthworms. It also will eat fallen fruit, berries, and eggs. The skunk probably is best known for its ability to cause an extremely unpleasant odor. When it is threatened and cannot get away, it ejects a strong-smelling fluid at its attacker. Few animals are willing to risk this attack, so skunks have few enemies. Probably more skunks are killed on highways by cars than by natural predators. The skunk is 32-46 cm (13-18 in) in length, with a tail 17-26 cm (7-10 in) long. The female striped skunk can have a litter of four to five young. It lives for about seven years.

Living Things of the Valley

Mule Deer (Mammal)

A shy animal, the mule deer lives in a variety of habitats. Adept at hiding, the mule deer is difficult to see. It browses on shoots and twigs of trees and grazes on grasses and shrubs. It also enjoys fallen fruit and nuts. The mule deer has large ears that move almost constantly as it listens for sounds. It has a stocky body, with long slim, sturdy legs. It is reddish-brown to grayish-brown in color, with a white throat and rump patch. The mule deer is 1.2-1.5 m (4-5 ft) long and weighs 115-140 kg (250-300 lb). The male deer antlers have a 80 cm (2.5 ft) span. Mountain lions, wolves, and coyotes are the deer's major enemies. Humans also hunt the mule deer for meat. The female mule deer gives birth in June to two fawns. It can have a lifespan of 10 years.

Opossum (Mammal)

This small gray creature has a long pointed nose, pinkish-white face, and a long naked tail. The opossum can usually be found out at night. It has a diverse diet of insects, fruit, eggs, frogs, birds, snakes, earthworms, rotten meat, and garbage scraps. The female opossum has six to nine babies and carries them around with her on her back. The opossum is hunted by humans for its fur and meat. The term "playing possum" comes from the opossum's ability to "play" dead when it is startled or threatened. It is 36-46 cm (15-18 in) in length. The life-span of the opossum is rarely longer than two years.

Mountain Lion (Mammal)

This beautiful and very secretive creature can be found in the mountains and valleys of our country. Long and lean, the mountain lion is immensely powerful and capable of killing large mammals, mainly deer. It can run very fast over short distances, but it tires quickly. The mountain lion usually hunts deer and other animals by rushing or by pouncing from trees and overhanging rocks. This cat species has tawny to gray fur with a long, dark-tipped tail. The female gives birth to two to six kittens in a carefully hidden den. It weighs between 70-100 kg (150-225 lb) and measures between 170-280 cm (5.5-9 ft) long. It lives up to 15 or more years in the wild.

Garter Snake (Reptile)

The common garter snake is the most widespread snake in United States. There are different subspecies, but most have three light stripes and a checkered pattern. It is often found near water such as a stream or pond. Garter snakes can be found living in large groups of several hundred individuals. The garter snake does not stun large prey with venom, nor does it coil around an animal, so it can prey only on small animals such as fish, frogs. salamanders, and earthworms. It averages in length 48-110 cm (1.5- 3.5 ft).

Rainbow Trout (Fish)

The rainbow trout, a native fish of the United States, is found in fast running, clear stream waters. It is a favorite of people who like to fish for sport because it is a fighter when caught on a hook and it is a good fish to eat. It eats mainly insects, small fish, tadpoles, and worms. It is about 30-90 cm (1- 3 ft) long and can weigh up to 9 kg (20 lb).

Living Things of the Valley

Barn Owl   (Bird)

The barn owl is a medium-sized owl with a white, heart-shaped face. It has a light golden brown body with long feathered legs. It flies on silent wings, appearing ghostly in the dim light at night. The barn owl is an efficient rodent killer, a farmer's ally. It depends mainly upon its ears to catch the small mammal prey. A barn owl does not digest fur and bone, it regurgitates them in the form of pellets. It is 32-50 cm (13-19 in) tall. The barn owl makes its nest in barns, buildings, or trees near open fields. There it lays four to seven white eggs. This owl only lives about two years.

Steller's Jay   (Bird)

Nicknamed "camp robbers," a Steller's jay is almost always present around a campground in the forest. A handsome, noisy bird, it is known for its loud calls. It has a beautiful blue color and perky crest that make the jay a very striking bird. The Steller's jay feeds on nuts, seeds, insects, birds' eggs, and small birds. It is about 30-32 cm (12-14 in) in length. It makes a well-hidden nest of twigs and grass where it lays three to five greenish eggs.

Crow   (Bird)

An intelligent bird, the crow is an inhabitant of the forests, valleys, and even the cities. It gathers in large numbers in areas associated with human activities — farmlands, rural road sides, and towns. The crow does a valuable service to humans in controlling insect populations. It measures up to 46 cm (18 in) in length and is entirely black. It builds a bowl-shaped nest where four to six greenish eggs are laid.

Red-Tailed Hawk   (Bird)

The red-tailed hawk can often be seen sitting on a fence post or on a telephone pole along the highway. The bright tail can easily be seen when the hawk is in flight. It hunts from the air or from its high perch, seeking the small mammals which provide the bulk of its diet. This hawk plays an important role in controlling the rodent population. A large bird, the red-tailed hawk is 48-62 cm (19-25 in) long and has a wingspan of 1.4 m (4.5 ft). It looks for a tall tree or cliff where it makes its nest and lays one to four white eggs.

Bald Eagle   (Bird)

This magnificent bird is one of North America's largest raptors. It has excellent eyesight, sharp talons on its feet for grasping and holding, and a powerful hooked beak with a sharp cutting edge to help tear its prey into bits. The bald eagle is not bald but has a white head, neck, and tail; the rest of its body is dark brown. It is a large bird, 76-102 cm (30-42 in) in length, with a wingspan of 2 m (7.5 ft). The eagle is found along rivers, lakes, and the seacoast where it feeds on fish, small mammals, and water fowl. It builds a massive stick nest in dead trees or on a cliff. There it will raise one to three babies each year.

Living Things of the Valley

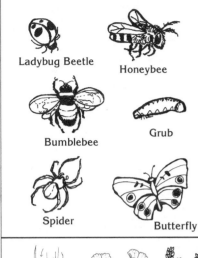

Ladybug Beetle

Honeybee

Bumblebee

Grub

Spider

Butterfly

Insects and Spiders

The insects of the valley have an important part in the food chain of the area. The **ladybug beetle** and its larvae are well known for their role in controlling aphids. They are easily recognized by their round, red, yellow, or orange bodies with black markings. Most ladybugs are 1-10 mm (0.06-0.35 in) long. The **honeybee** is important for the pollination of plants and the production of honey. This insect, 15-17 mm (0.65 in) in length, can usually be seen at flowers. The **bumble-bee** is a large bee, 10-20 mm (0.75 in) long. Its large hairy, yellow, and black body can usually be seen at flowers. The **grub**, a larva of the beetles, is a favorite food of the bears who hunt in the meadows and under logs to find them. Many different kinds of **butterflies** can be seen collecting nectar from the flowers. Several different varieties of **spiders** make their home among the grasses and plants and provide food for the birds.

California Poppy

Lupine

Blue-Eyed Grass

Flowers and Grasses

Blue-eyed grasses, the golden-colored blossoms of the **California poppies,** and the blue blossoms of the **Lupine** represent just three of the multitude of wildflowers that grow in the valley. **Grasses** predominate as the vegetation that provides food for the grazing animals.

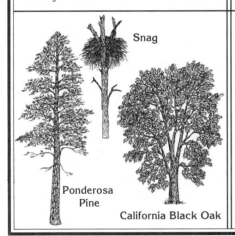

Snag

Ponderosa Pine

California Black Oak

Trees

One of the most common and important timber trees is the **Ponderosa Pine.** It grows to a height of 48-55 m (150-180 ft). It has brown bark with large flat plates. The green needles grow in groups of two to three and are 10-28 cm (4-11 in) long. The **California Black Oak** grows in the drier portions of the area and in the grasslands. The acorns of the oaks in the area are a staple in the diet of many birds, squirrels, bears, and deer. The black oak grows to a height of 15-18 m (50-60 ft). The **snag,** or dead tree, is very important as a place for a multitude of living things to reside. It often supports eagles' and woodpeckers' nests, holes in the trunk become squirrels' residence, and many insects burrow into the bark.

Living Things of the Valley

Living Things	Home	Food	Characteristics
Mammals			
Black Bear	Valleys, mountains, forests	Berries, plants, fish, small animals, insects	Omnivorous; black body; brown nose; hibernates in winter; 1.2-1.8 m (4-6 ft) long; 0.6-0.9 m (2-3 ft) tall at shoulder; 95-230 kg (200-500 lb)
Bobcat	Valleys, mountains	Rodents, rabbits, squirrels	Tawny color; stumpy tail; tufted ears; rarely seen; 60-110 cm (25-42 in); 6-12 kg (13-25 lb)
Badger	Valleys, mountains	Plants, worms, insects, rodents	Gray, flattened body; strong front feet for digging; 44-60 cm (18-22 in); 9-17 kg (20-36 lb)
Chipmunk	Forests, rocky areas	Nuts, seeds, berries, insects, slugs	Reddish-brown; tail as long as small, slim body; hibernates in winter; 9-11 cm (3.5-4.5 in)
Elk	Mountain meadows, forests	Grasses, plants	Large brown animal; light colored rump; large rack of antlers; male sheds antlers yearly; 2.4-3 m (7.5-9.5 ft)
Gray Fox	Forests	Rodents, rabbits, fruit, plants	Climbs trees; gray fur with reddish bands; bushy tail; hunts at night; 60-75 cm (2-2.5 ft); 1.9-6 kg (4-13 lb)
Porcupine	Forests, valleys	Leaves, twigs, bark of tree	Chunky body; short legs; thousands of quills; yellowish-brown; spends much time in trees; 46-65 cm (18-26 in); 4.8-13 kg (10-25 lb)
Striped Skunk	Forests, valleys, suburbs	Beetles, insects, vegetation	Black and white striped; protects itself by spraying a bad-smelling fluid; 32-46 cm (13-18 in)
Mule Deer	Forests, wooded valleys	Shrubs, twigs, grasses, fruit, nuts	Tan coat; large ears; black-tipped tail; males shed antlers yearly; 1.2-1.5 m (4-5 ft); 50-215 kg (110-475 lb) male; 32-73 kg (70-160 lb) female

Living Things of the Valley

Living Things	Home	Food	Characteristics
Opossum	Valleys, suburbs	Insects, fruits	Grayish fur; white face; naked, rat-like tail; "plays dead" (playing possum); 36-46 cm (15-18 in)
Mountain Lion	Mountains, forests	Deer, other mammals	Often called a cougar; tawny color; 170-280 cm (5.5-9 ft); 70-100 kg (150-225 lb)
Reptile			
Garter Snake	Near water	Fish, frogs, earth-worms, salamanders	Found all over US; not venom-ous; 48-110 cm (1.5-3.5 ft)
Fish			
Rainbow Trout	Clear, fast, stream water	Insects, small fish, worms	Good fish to eat; 30-90 cm (1-3 ft); up to 9 kg (20 lb)
Birds			
Barn Owl	Open country	Rodents, small birds	Medium-sized; white, heart-shaped face; golden-brown body; regurgitates pellets; 32-50 cm (13-19 in) tall
Steller's Jay	Forested, open area	Seeds, nuts, insects	Noisy; blue bird; crested; found near campgrounds; 30-32 cm (12-14 in)
Crow	Forests, fields, suburbs	Insects, seeds	Black bird; thick black bill; call is a caw; 46 cm (18 in)
Red-Tailed Hawk	Open fields, forests	Rodents, small mammals	Dark, broad-winged; wide, red tail; 48-62 cm (19-25 in) long; 1.4 m (4.5 ft) wingspan
Bald Eagle	Rivers, forests	Fish, birds, rodents	Large dark bird; white head and tail; yellow legs and bill; 76-102 cm (30-42 in) long; 2 m (7.5 ft) wingspan

Living Things of the Valley

Living Things	Home	Food	Characteristics
Insects			
Ladybug Beetle	Valley, brushy area	Aphids	Shiny red, orange, yellow with black markings; a predator; 1-10 mm (0.06-0.35 in)
Honeybee	At flowers	Nectar, honey	Yellow-brown with black; used to pollinate crops and produce honey; 15-17 mm (0.65 in)
Bumblebee	At flowers	Nectar, honey	Yellow and black; large, robust; hairy; 10-20 mm (0.75 in)
Butterfly	Valleys	Nectar, pollen	Various colors and patterns; 5-8 cm (2-3 in)
Invertebrate			
Spider	Grasses	Small insects	Provides food for birds; less than 1 cm (1/4-1/2 m)
Trees			
Ponderosa Pine	Mountain sides		Important timber tree; 48-55 m (150-180 ft) tall; needles 10-28 cm (4-11 in)
California Black Oak	In valley		Grows in drier areas of valley; acorns are staple diet of many birds and animals; 15-18 m (50-60 ft)

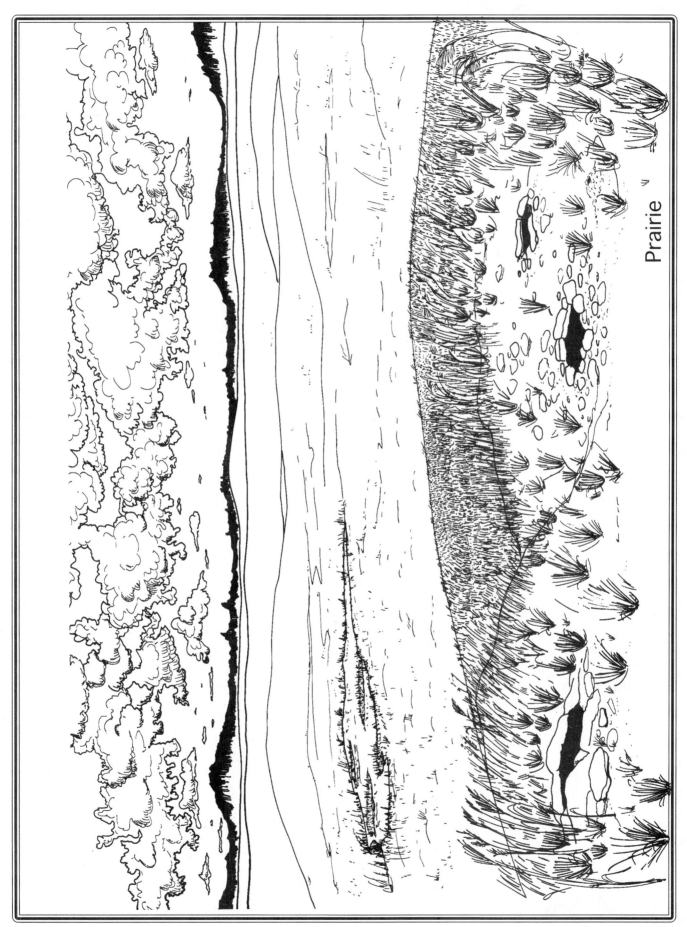

Prairie

Prairies

The prairie, a broad region of flat or gently rolling land covered with grasses, was often described by the pioneers as "grass as far as the eye can see." Few natural prairie grass areas remain, most of the land is now used for farming wheat and corn. The North American prairie extends from central Canada down through the central states to Texas.

Weather on the prairies varies widely throughout the year. The summers can be hot with temperatures over 38°C (100°F), followed by cold winters where blizzards howl down the plains and temperatures plunge well below -20°C (0°F). Precipitation averages 50 cm (20+ inches) a year. Most of the moisture falls in the late spring and early summer. It is in this area that the clash of cold air from the north and warm moist air from the Gulf can result in very severe weather and often thunder and lightning storms can form. Tornadoes are dangerous storms that also can form from this conflict between the two air masses.

Most prairie soils are rich, deep, and dark. These come from the soil deposited by the glaciers and from the growth and decay of deep grass roots. The rich soil supports thick stands of grasses and productive farmland. The big and little bluestem and the tough buffalo grass are some of the many native grasses.

Plants other than grasses also grow on the prairie. Species of flowers such as the scarlet globe mallow, blazing star, sunflowers, and asters make splashes of red, yellow, purple, and other colors in the sea of grass. Cattails, sedges, and some trees such as the cottonwoods and willows grow near rivers or ponds.

Animals are especially numerous on the prairie. Large herds of bison, commonly called buffaloes, formerly roamed the prairies and fed on the grasses. Hunters in the late 1800s slaughtered hundreds of thousands of these animals. Most bison are now found on game preserves. Jack rabbits, pronghorns, and deer browse on the grasses. They usually live in family groups, herds, or packs to help each other. Many plant-eating creatures feed on the leaves, roots, and seeds of the grasses. Birds, mice, and prairie dogs eat the seeds of the plants and nest in the grasses or live underground in burrows.

The carnivores, or meat-eating animals — coyotes, foxes, skunks, and bull snakes — feed on the smaller prairie animals. Hawks, falcons, and owls are meat-eating birds that also feast on these small animals.

Insects are numerous, such as the grasshopper, monarch butterflies, and ants. Many species of birds gain part of their food from these insects. The prairie chicken, meadowlark, quail, and sparrows are some of the many kind of birds found on the prairies.

The pioneers found that the black prairie soil was rich in humus, deep, and very fertile and made superior farmland. So the sod of the prairie was plowed and the land turned into cropland. The prairie land of the mid-west is now used extensively for growing grains, cattle, and field crops.

Prairie

grayish-brown
with white
underside

Coyote

brown black
tan

Bull Snake

golden tan with
white underside

Prairie Dogs

Science Buddy

Prairie

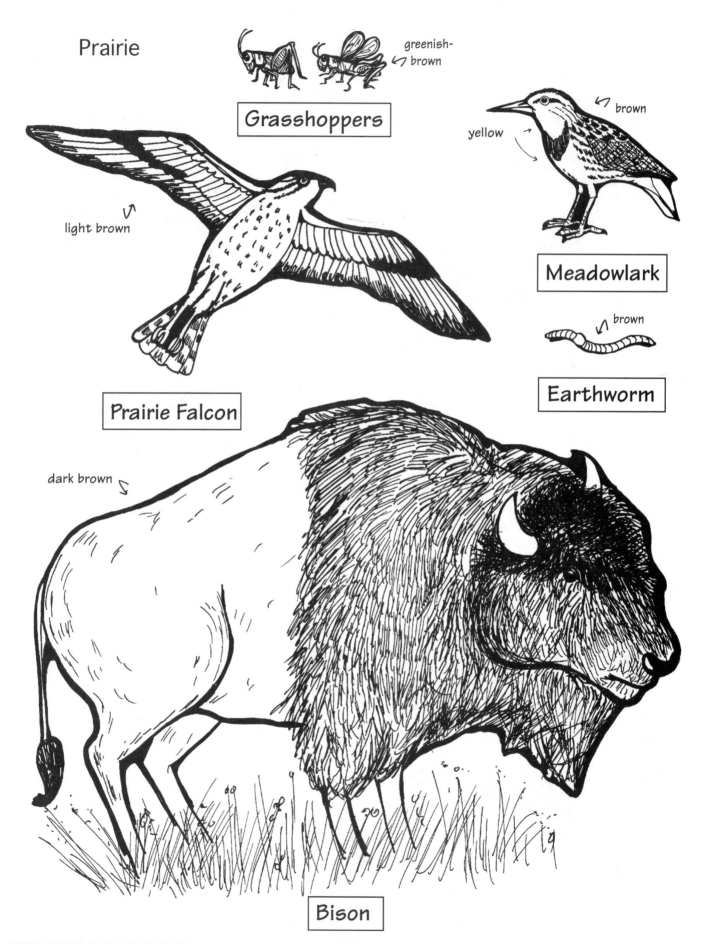

Grasshoppers

greenish-brown

Meadowlark

brown

yellow

brown

Earthworm

light brown

Prairie Falcon

dark brown

Bison

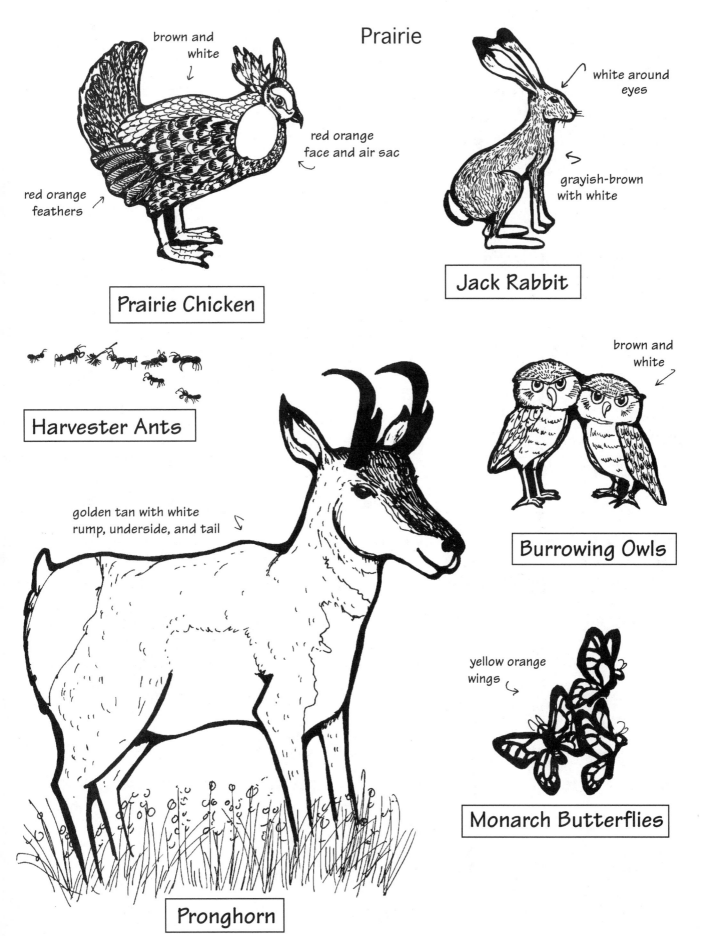

Prairie

brown and
white

red orange
face and air sac

red orange
feathers

Prairie Chicken

white around
eyes

grayish-brown
with white

Jack Rabbit

Harvester Ants

brown and
white

Burrowing Owls

golden tan with white
rump, underside, and tail

yellow orange
wings

Monarch Butterflies

Pronghorn

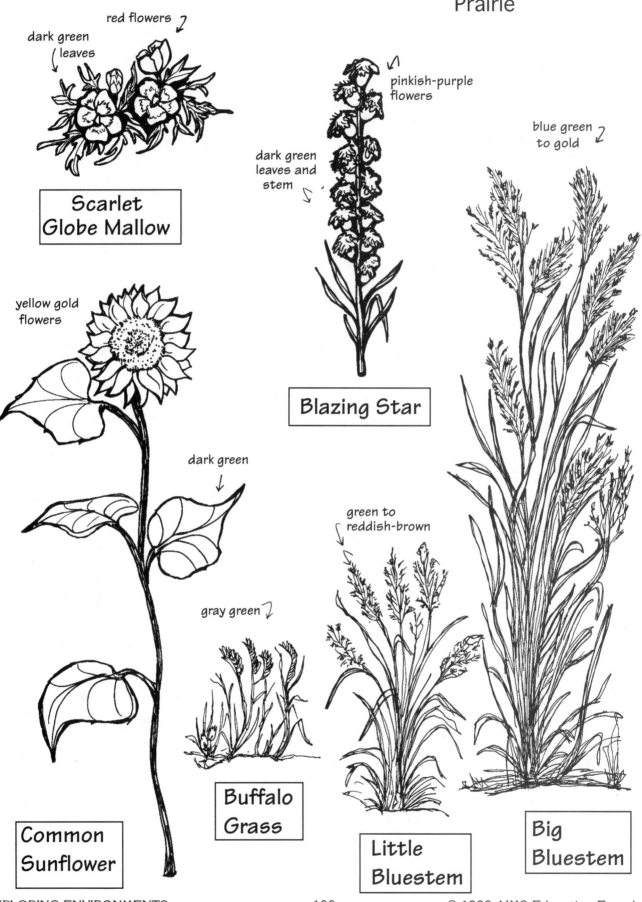

red flowers

dark green leaves

Scarlet Globe Mallow

pinkish-purple flowers

dark green leaves and stem

Blazing Star

blue green to gold

yellow gold flowers

dark green

gray green

green to reddish-brown

Common Sunflower

Buffalo Grass

Little Bluestem

Big Bluestem

Living Things of the Prairie

	**Bullsnake** **(Reptile)** A large, powerfully built snake, 1.2-2.4 m (4-8 ft) long, the bullsnake lives in the brushes and grasses of the prairies. It can be found under rocks or in burrows. It eats rodents and bird eggs. Like other constrictors, it wraps its brown and black body around its prey and squeezes. When disturbed, the bullsnake hisses loudly and lunges at the intruder. During the summer the female bullsnake will lay clutches of 3-24 eggs in sandy burrows or beneath logs. The eggs hatch in two to two and a half months.
	**Coyote** **(Mammal)** The haunting song of the coyote can often be heard at night. This is the animal's way of communicating with others of its kind. Tough, wiry, and with keen senses, the coyote adapts to almost any habitat. It can be found almost any place in the United States, even in and around cities. The coyote feeds mainly on rodents, rabbits, and other small animals. It is 100 to 130 cm (40-50 in) long and weighs 9 to 23 kg (20 to 50 lbs). The coyote is grayish-brown with tan legs and feet. It can run 40-50 km/h (25-30 mph). In the spring, the female will produce a litter of about six pups on the average. Most coyotes live only six to eight years in the wild.
	**Prairie Dog** **(Mammal)** The prairie dog is a rodent with a broad head and a fat, golden-brown body. It lives in colonies called prairie dog towns. The town consists of elaborate tunnels which sometimes are several feet below the surface of the ground. It is called a prairie dog because of its warning bark which sounds like a dog's bark. It is 30-50 cm (12-20 in) long. It eats grasses and weedy plants. Three to five babies are born to the prairie dog each year. The average life span of the prairie dog is seven to eight years.
	**Pronghorn** **(Mammal)** One of the fastest animals on the prairie, the antelope can outdistance almost all its predators. It can run nearly 65 km/h (40 mph) and leap 6 m (20 ft) in one jump. The pronghorn is a tan animal, with two white stripes on its breast and white on its sides and rump. The white hairs on the pronghorn's rump are raised as a warning signal to other members of its herd. This signal can be seen from over 3 km (2 mi) away. It stands 90 cm (3 ft) at the shoulders and weighs about 41-68 kg (90-150 lbs). It grazes on the grass, wildflowers, and shrubs of the prairie. Two fawns are born to the female pronghorn in the spring. In about three weeks the fawns are able to eat grass and shrubs. The life span of the pronghorn is up to ten years.

Living Things of the Prairie

Bison (Buffalo)   (Mammal)
A large male bison may weigh 900 kg (2,000 lb). Most of its massive weight is concentrated in its forequarters. Its large low-slung head is supported by a heavily muscled neck. Its head has horns on the side that point upward. It is a dark brown color and has a shaggy mane and beard. It has a long tail with a tuft on the end, short legs, and large hoofs. It is 2 m (6 ft) tall and 3 m (10 ft) long. It is a surprisingly fast runner for its size and can swim well. The bison was an important part of the Native Americans' way of life. They ate its meat, used its skin for clothing and shelter, and its bones for tools. This large, shaggy creature once roamed through all of the prairie lands feeding on native grasses, but it was hunted nearly to extinction. Every two years, the female bison will produce a calf that weighs about 30 kg (65 lbs). The life span in the wild averages 25 years.

Jack Rabbit   (Mammal)
The jack rabbit is noted for it very long ears. A grayish-brown rabbit with very large hind feet, it is 40-60 cm (16-24 in) in length and weighs 1.8-3.6 kg (4-8 lbs). The jack rabbit eats alfalfa and other grasses. It is a fast runner and can leap 6 m (20 ft). Coyotes, owls, hawks, and bobcats are the jack rabbit's predators. The female jack rabbit can have up to six babies in each litter, but she can have three to four litters a year. Few jack rabbits live more than one year.

Prairie Chicken   (Bird)
The prairie chicken is well known for the male's courtship display. Two orange air sacs on the side of the male bird's neck are inflated during courtship and help him give loud booming calls. The prairie chicken lives in an area with long grasses in which it can nest. Grains, nuts, tree buds, leaves, and insects make up the normal diet of this bird. It is brown and white in color and is 40-45 cm (16-18 in) in length. In a grass-lined nest among the tall grasses, the prairie chicken lays 11-13 buff-colored eggs.

Prairie Falcon   (Bird)
The prairie falcon can be seen flying over the dry plains and prairies. It usually nests on high rocky ledges. Its staple foods are ground squirrels, rodents, and birds. It has a spectacular dive to catch its prey. A light brown bird with a creamy white breast, the prairie falcon nests on a protected cliff ledge where it lays three to six reddish eggs. It is 42-50 cm (17-20 in) long with pointed wings and a long tail.

Burrowing Owls   (Bird)
A mottled brown and white bird of prey, the burrowing owl is found mainly on the open land. It is most often seen during the day standing on its long legs near its nesting site. The burrowing owl makes its home in abandoned rodent burrows where it lays five to seven white eggs. It eats mostly insects and rodents which it catches usually at night. The bird stands 20-25 cm (8-10 in) tall.

Living Things of the Prairie

	Meadowlark (Bird) This is a popular brown-colored bird with a yellow breast and a V-shaped black bib. It is well known for its loud cheerful song given when perching on fences or posts. The meadowlark is 20-26 cm (8-10 in) long. It feeds on insects and seeds. The meadowlark lays three to seven heavily spotted eggs in a grassy nest.
	Harvester Ants (Insect) The harvester ant is a social insect that lives in a communal nest with thousands of others, each with a task to perform. The ant is a dark reddish-brown, wingless (except when swarming) insect that averages 6-13 mm (0.25-0.50 in) in length. It eats mainly seeds and grains, but a colony of harvester ants can cause severe damage to crops by cutting down plants and creating bare spots in a field.
	Grasshoppers (Insect) The grasshopper is easily recognized by the long, powerful hind legs that are used for jumping. This greenish-brown insect has a large flat-sided head with big compound eyes and large chewing mouth. The grasshopper is known for the musical sounds made when it rubs together portions of its legs or wings. It is a troublesome agricultural pest which destroys crops when it descends on fields in huge swarms to eat the foliage. It is 2.5-5 cm (1-2 in) in length. Grasshoppers usually live just one year. The female grasshopper lays large masses of 8-25 eggs below the surface of the ground.
	Monarch Butterflies (Insect) The monarch is a large, brightly colored orange and black butterfly. Its larvae feed on the milkweed plant. The monarch butterfly is the only one that migrates like birds do. It winters in Mexico and California and flies as far north as Canada in the summer. It has a wingspan of 7.5-10 cm (3-4 in). Each female monarch lays about 400 clear green oval eggs on the underside of a milkweed leaf. Monarch butterflies which are born in early spring and summer live only a few weeks; those born in late autumn are the generation that migrates and they will live for eight or nine months.
	Earthworm (Invertebrate) The earthworm is a very common but important part of the environment. It is a long, segmented, soft-bodied animal. It ranges in length from 2.5-20 cm (1-8 in) and is usually brown in color. The earthworm can be found in moist soil which it aerates with its burrows and fertilizes with its castings. It feeds on decaying plant material.

Living Things of the Prairie

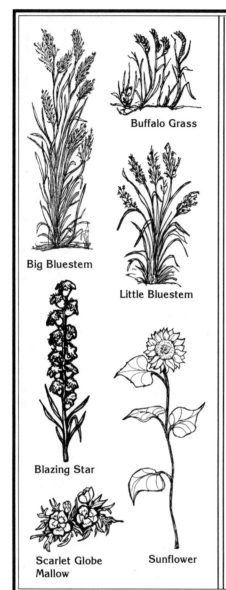

Buffalo Grass

Big Bluestem

Little Bluestem

Blazing Star

Scarlet Globe
Mallow

Sunflower

Prairie Plants (Plant)

Buffalo grass is one of the most important forage grasses of the prairies. It has underground runners that helps to form soil-binding sod. This was often used by the early settlers to make their sod houses.

The **big and little bluestem** are the dominant plants in the prairie. They have ribbonlike green leaves with gold to brown colored bracts.

The **blazing star** is a wildflower that greeted the pioneers as they crossed the prairies. This thistle-like flower is a beautiful pinkish-purple color.

The **scarlet globe mallow** is a brick-red flower that can be found on the dry grasslands of the prairies.

The striking bright yellow flower of the **common sunflower** is quite evident on the prairie because it grows atop a stout stem and it turns to face the sun. It has a flowerhead with petal-like, yellow-ray flowers around a flat brownish central disk.

Living Things of the Prairie

Living Things	Home	Food	Characteristics
Reptiles			
Bullsnake	In grasses and around rocks	Rodents, bird eggs	A constrictor; eats mice, rats in burrows; 1.2-2.4 m (4-8 ft)
Mammals			
Coyote	Wooded and open areas	Small animals such as rodents and rabbits	Grayish-brown; hunts largely at night; fast; clever; has sharp teeth; 100-130 cm (40-50 in)
Prairie Dog	Underground burrows in the grasslands	Seeds, grass	Stocky, short-tailed ground squirrel; light brown; barks a warning call; eaten by coyotes, falcons, bobcats; 30-50 cm (12-20 in)
Pronghorn	Grasslands	Leaves, grasses, and shrubs	Fast runner; roams from Canada to Mexico; tall at shoulder; large ears; slender legs; short tail; eaten by coyotes and wolves; 90 cm (3 ft)
Bison (Buffalo)	Grasslands	Grasses	Large head; shaggy fur; 2 m (6 ft) tall; 3 m (10 ft) long; 900 kg (2000 lb); eaten by wolves and coyotes
Jack Rabbit	Grasslands	Grass, green plants	Big ears; large hind feet; fast runner; leaps 6 m (20 ft); ears pick up sounds and cool body; 40-60 cm (16-24 in)
Birds			
Prairie Chicken	Tall grass, prairie	Seeds, insects	Male uses orange air sacs, neck feathers, and tail to attract female; deep booming voice; 40-45 cm (16-18 in)

Living Things of the Prairie

Living Things	Home	Food	Characteristics
Prairie Falcon	High rocky ledges, open areas	Small birds	Pointed wings; long tail; spectacular dives to catch prey; 42-50 cm (17-20 in)
Burrowing Owls	In burrows, open areas	Insects, reptiles, rodents	Long legs; short tail; nests in abandoned prairie dog burrows; seen often at entrance to burrow; 20-25 cm (8-10 in)
Meadowlark	Meadows, open areas	Insects	Black V across yellow breast; beautiful song; 20-26 cm (8-10 in)
Insects			
Harvester Ants	Fields, sandy areas	Seeds, grains	Damages crops; painful bite; brown; 6-13 mm (0.25-0.50 in)
Grasshoppers	Grasslands	Grasses	Destructive to crops; leaps or flies; 2.5-5 cm (1-2 in)
Monarch Butterflies	Fields, grasslands, open areas	Larvae feed on the milkweed plant	Migratory, winters in Mexico and California; brown and orange wings; 7.5-10 cm (3-4 in)
Invertebrate			
Earthworm	Prairie soil	Decaying plant material	Soft bodied; segmented; no legs; 2.5-20 cm (1-8 in)

Living Things of the Prairie

Living Things	Home	Color	Characteristics
Plants			
Buffalo Grass	Plains, prairies	Gray-green leaves	Spreading plants; sod-forming; blooms May-August; 5-15 cm (2-6 in)
Big and Little Bluestem	Prairies, fields	Gold to brown colored bracts	Dominant plants in the prairie areas; blooms June-October; big bluestem is 5-20 cm (2-8 in); little bluestem is 2.5-10 cm (1-4 in)
Blazing Star	Dry prairies	Pinkish-purple flowers	Thistle-like; blooms August-October; 6-10 cm (1-4 in)
Scarlet Globe Mallow	Dry grasslands	Red flowers with pale centers	Hairy leaves; blooms May-August; 2.5-6 cm (1-2 in)
Common Sunflower	Dry prairies	Yellow ray flowers around a brown center	Flowerhead 7.5-25 cm (3-10 in) diameter; 0.6-3.8 m (2-12 ft) tall

Desert

Desert Lands

A desert is a region that receives less than 25 cm (10 in) of moisture each year. Deserts have many different landscapes and types of soil. Sand and sand dunes cover about one-fourth of the desert land; gravel and rock-covered hills, mountains, and lowlands cover the rest. Deep gullies and washes which crisscross the landscape are the result of infrequent downpours that wash across the land and scour soil and rocks from the landscape. Most of the streams are seasonal and flow only during times when a large amount of rain or snow is received.

The plant and animal life that are able to live in these harsh environments have adjusted to these conditions. Many kinds of plants and animals flourish in the desert. Desert plants have adapted to the extreme dryness of the weather in various ways. Some have roots that go down in the Earth a hundred feet or more, others have roots that spread out horizontally. Other plants store large amounts of water in their leaves, roots, or stems. The individual plants tend to be spaced widely so they can compete for the small amount of water available. Quite often a desert area will receive no rainfall for years, then a big storm will release a brief, violent downpour of rain. Many wildflowers will grow and bloom in a very short time after a rain.

A surprisingly large number of animals, insects, reptiles, birds, and spiders live in the desert. Most desert animals stay in shady areas and remain inactive during the day to stay cool and to conserve the moisture in their bodies. Many dig burrows and stay underground during the day, coming out at night to hunt and feed. Desert animals quite often obtain water from the food they eat and from the few areas that have water holes.

It is the smaller animals that seem to survive under these harsh conditions. Larger animals, like deer, wolves, and foxes, do not live in the desert areas but visit in search of food.

Deserts include some of the hottest places on Earth. The desert land absorbs more heat from the sun than more humid areas. Desert temperatures often reach 38°C (100°F) or higher during the day and may drop to 10°C (50°F) at night.

Deserts cannot support large numbers of people and animals. Many desert soils are rich in salt, uranium, gold, and other minerals and in some areas oil and natural gas. But humans have had to make many adjustments in order to reap the rewards of mining these minerals.

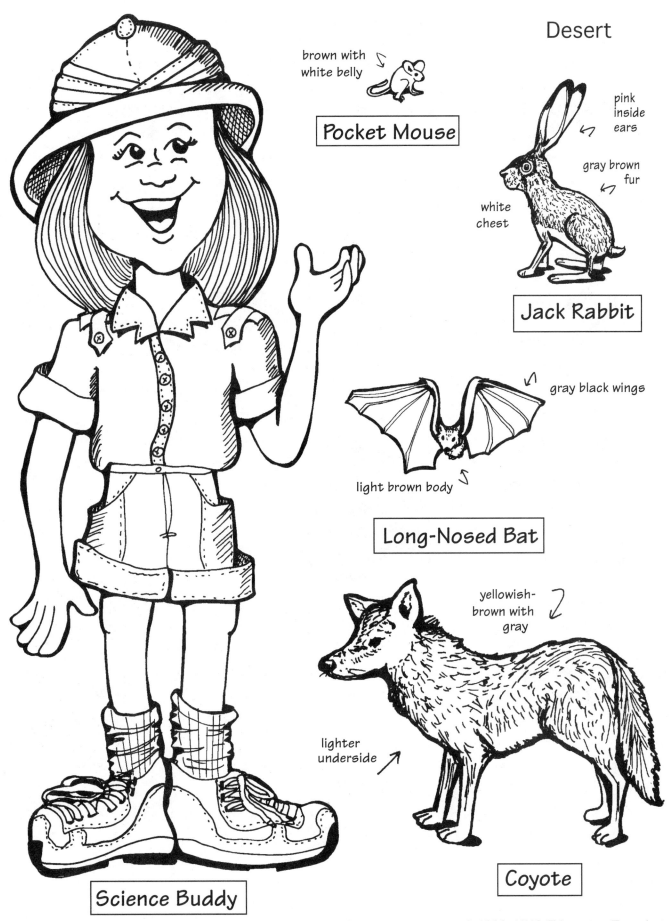

Desert

brown with white belly

Pocket Mouse

pink inside ears

gray brown fur

white chest

Jack Rabbit

gray black wings

light brown body

Long-Nosed Bat

yellowish-brown with gray

lighter underside

Coyote

Science Buddy

Desert

gray
and tan

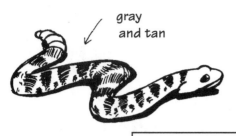

Sidewinder

orange and black

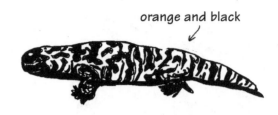

Gila Monster

green with
white
spots

brown head

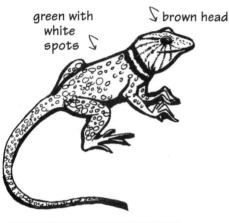

Collared Lizard

tan gray

Horned Toad

brown

Desert Tortoise

light brown body
with yellowish legs

Scorpion

dark brown

Tarantula

Tarantula Hawk

Ants

Desert

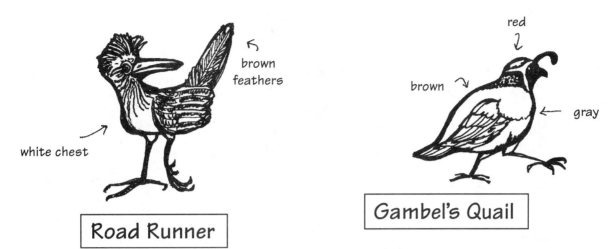

brown
feathers

white chest

Road Runner

red

brown

gray

Gambel's Quail

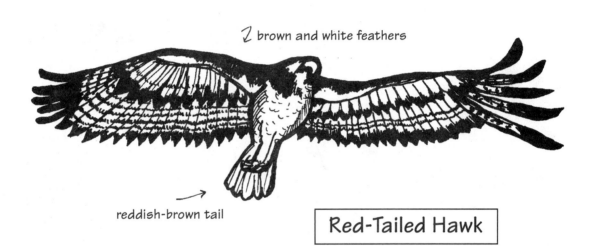

⟋ brown and white feathers

reddish-brown tail

Red-Tailed Hawk

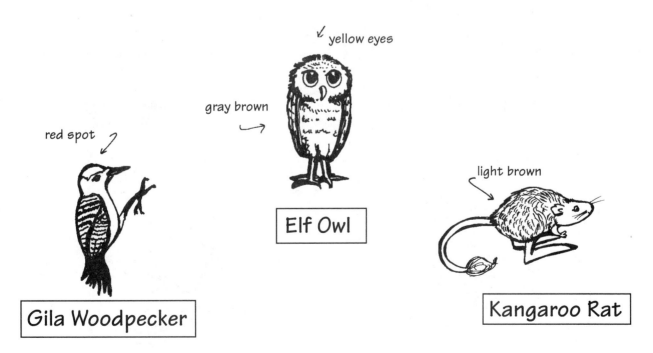

yellow eyes

gray brown

red spot

light brown

Elf Owl

Gila Woodpecker

Kangaroo Rat

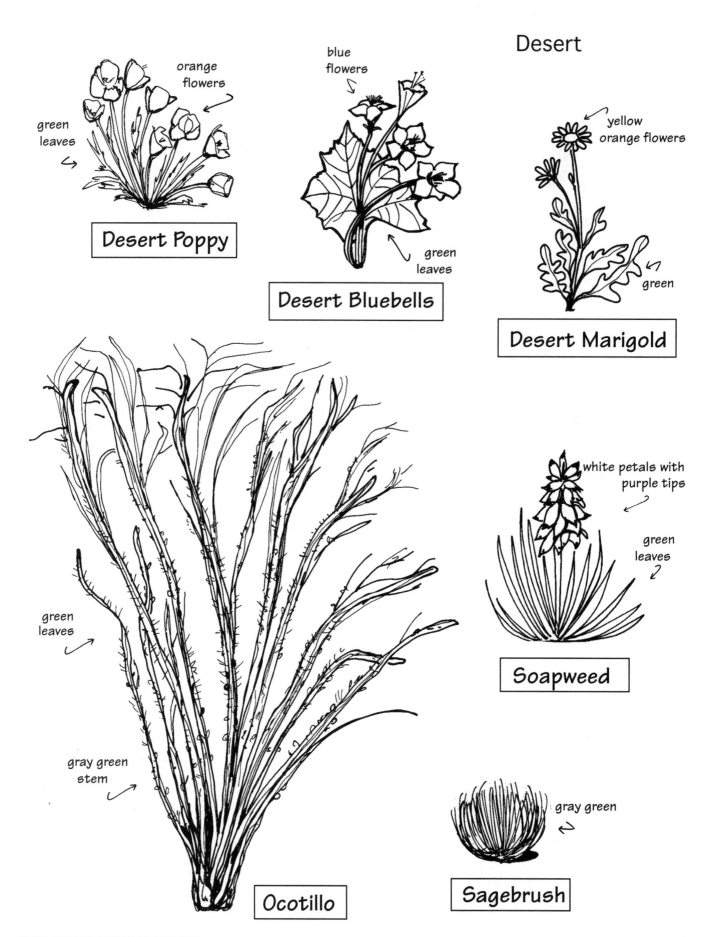

Desert

orange flowers

green leaves

Desert Poppy

blue flowers

green leaves

Desert Bluebells

yellow orange flowers

green

Desert Marigold

white petals with purple tips

green leaves

Soapweed

green leaves

gray green stem

Ocotillo

gray green

Sagebrush

113

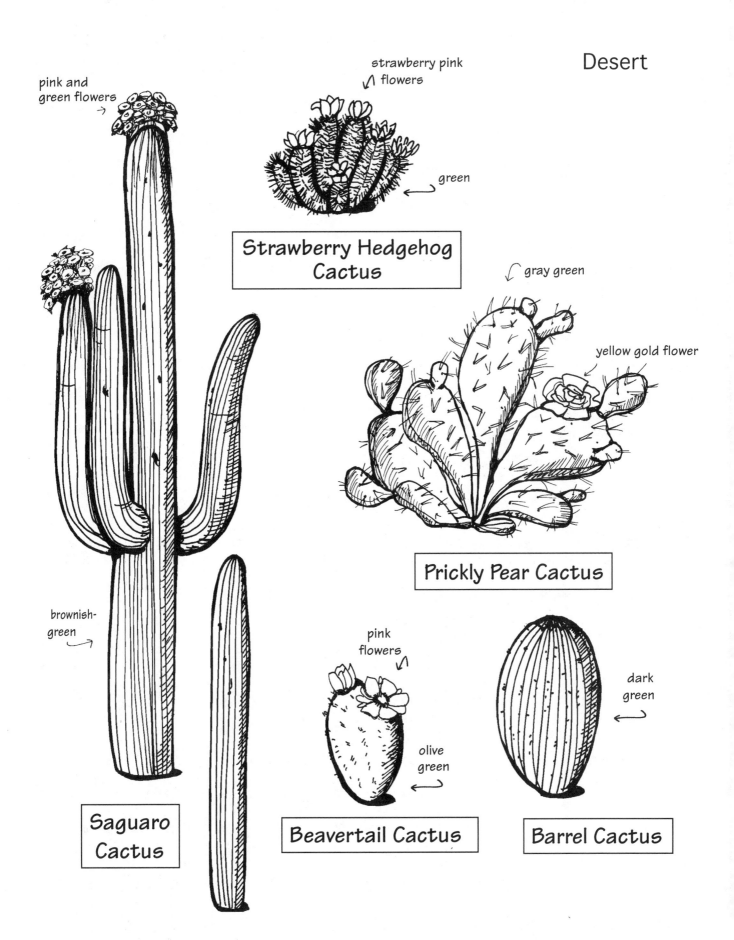

pink and green flowers

strawberry pink flowers

green

Strawberry Hedgehog Cactus

gray green

yellow gold flower

Prickly Pear Cactus

brownish-green

pink flowers

dark green

olive green

Saguaro Cactus

Beavertail Cactus

Barrel Cactus

Living Things of the Desert

Long-Nosed Bat   (Mammal)

The long-nosed bat lives in the desert where it feeds on the nectar of cactus flowers. This light brown creature uses its long nose and tongue to reach deep into a cactus flower to eat the nectar, and in the process, it pollinates the plant. It is especially attracted to the blossoms of the saguaro cactus. The long-nosed bat can be found hanging upside down in crevices and caves during the day. The tiny animal which can live up to 15 years has a mass of only 30 grams (1 oz). The female bat gives birth to one baby in the spring.

Jack Rabbit   (Mammal)

With its powerful hind legs, large ears, and bulging eyes, the jack rabbit is well built for life in the desert. It is a very fleet creature, able to escape from predators at speeds of 50-60 km/h (30 to 35 mph). Its strong hind legs help the jack rabbit to leap distances as great as 6 m (20 ft). It is a large rabbit averaging 60 cm (2 ft) in length which includes a 10 cm (4 in) tail. During the day the rabbit lies in shallow, shaded depressions. Its large ears act like antennas to detect enemies. The ears are also their "air conditioners" — wind blowing over the blood vessels in the ears cools the animal. Grasses, leaves, twigs of bushes, and the fruit of the cacti provide food for this desert animal. The jack rabbit has three to four litters a year, each time having up to six babies.

Coyote   (Mammal)

The coyote perhaps is best known in the desert areas for its "serenades." It has a series of barks and howls that echo over the evening landscape. The adult coyote measures about 1.2 m (4 ft) long, stands about 60 cm (2 ft) tall, and weighs 11-14 kg (25-30 lb). It has large erect ears, a pointed nose, slender legs, and a long bushy tail. It resembles a large dog. The coyote is not very particular about its diet; rabbits, mice, rats, and squirrels make up the bulk of what it eats, but insects and reptiles are also eaten, as are larger animals. A litter of 2-12 young are born to the coyote. It usually lives four years in the wild.

Kangaroo Rat   (Mammal)

This is an animal that has adapted to the dry desert; it can live without any drinking water. The kangaroo rat gets its water from the plants and seeds it eats. In some cases, its body will actually produce water. It has also adopted a nocturnal lifestyle, staying in its underground burrow during the day when the temperature is high and the humidity is low. It feeds at night when it is cooler and there is more moisture in the air. The kangaroo rat is a long-legged leaper. It can cover 60 cm (2 ft) in a single leap. It measures 10-12 cm (4-4.5 in) in length with a tail 13-15 cm (5-6 in) that is longer than its body. It feeds mainly on grasses and seeds. The female rat has one to two litters a year of one to six young. The kangaroo rat lives only about one year.

Living Things of the Desert

Pocket Mouse   (Mammal)

The pocket mouse is named for its habit of carrying seeds to its burrow in an expandable pouch on the outside of its cheeks. A relatively large mouse, it measures 11-13 cm (4.5-5 in) in length. It lives in a burrow dug under the bushes and is active mainly at night to escape the high daytime temperatures. Two to eight young are born to the mother mouse. Seeds constitute the bulk of its diet. The pocket mouse provides food for many desert creatures such as owls, coyotes, roadrunners, and hawks. The pocket mouse seldom lives more than a couple of months.

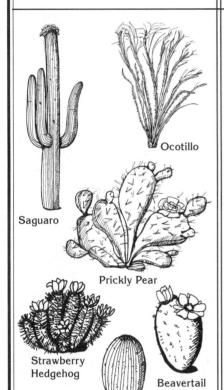

Ocotillo

Saguaro

Prickly Pear

Strawberry Hedgehog

Beavertail

Barrel

Cactus   (Plant)

This is a family of plants that can live in an area that receives very little rainfall. Cacti have very long roots that can gather in the infrequent water from rain. The roots either grow very deeply or spread very widely. They usually have clusters of spines on the body of the cacti that have replaced the leaves. Cacti are important to many animals of the desert. Small animals, insects, and birds feed on the stems of cacti. Many birds build nests among the thorns of the cacti, and other birds and animals hide from enemies in the thorns.

Perhaps the best known cactus is the **saguaro**, which may reach a height of 18 m (60 ft) and a diameter of 60 cm (2 ft). Flowers bloom on the tips of its branches. It is a very slow growing plant, taking 50-100 years to grow arms. Many of the saguaro cacti are several hundred years old.

The **ocotillo** is a branchless bouquet of thorny, whiplike stems. After a rain, this plant grows green leaves and produces showy red flowers on the end of its stems.

The **barrel** cactus is shaped like a barrel and has tough, curved spines. It may grow to 3 m (10 ft) tall. It is known for its juicy pulp that can be used as an emergency water source.

The **prickly pear** cactus has thorny leaf-like stems that have been flattened into oval pads. The plant bears pear-shaped fruit that are good to eat.

The **strawberry hedgehog** cactus is a plant 2.5-30 cm (1-12 in) tall with upright stems and showy red to maroon flowers.

The **beavertail** cactus has a stem that is shaped like a beavertail. The plant is topped with pink flowers in the spring.

Desert Bluebells

Desert Poppy

Soapweed

Desert Marigold

Flowers   (Plant)

With the coming of the spring, the desert blooms with a blaze of color. When the rain and sun are plentiful, the sandy flats and hillsides are covered with a carpet of flowers. The orange of the **desert poppy** and **desert marigold**, blue of the **desert bluebells**, and white of the **soapweed** are just a few of the wildflowers that brighten the desert scene.

Sagebrush   (Plant)

One of the dominant forms of vegetation in the desert is the sagebrush. This gray-green bush provides perches, shade, and food for many desert animals. It also keeps the soil from being washed or blown away by the weather. The sagebrush can grow 60-150 cm (2-5 ft) in height. It has yellow or white flowers and small leaves.

Living Things of the Desert

Sidewinder (Reptile)

The sidewinder is a rattlesnake that travels over loose sand in a looping S-curve, leaving a series of J-shaped parallel gouges behind. The sidewinder balances itself on it head and tail and then moves its midsection, leaving a record of its movement in the sand. This movement gives good traction and also lessens the surface area of the snake's body that is in contact with the sand. A small poisonous snake, only 45 cm (18 in) long, the sidewinder feeds on rodents, lizards, frogs, and insects. It is a favorite food of the roadrunner. The female sidewinder gives birth to 5-18 live young snakes.

Gila Monster (Reptile)

One of the few venomous reptiles in the desert other than snakes, the Gila monster roams the Sonoran Desert. It prefers the areas that have few shrubs. It lives under rocks or in burrows that it has taken from some rodent. In this burrow three to five eggs are laid in the fall. When it is cold the Gila monster hibernates in its burrow living on the fat it has stored in its tail. It has a squat, heavy body with a large head and a short thick tail. It has short sharp claws that it uses to dig up eggs of tortoises and to dig into the nests of rodents for its meals. It is 45 cm (18 in) long and weighs 1.4-2.3 kg (3-5 lb). The Gila monster's orange, black, and yellow skin markings and the texture of its granular skin camouflage the animal in its desert surroundings of sand and rocks.

Horned Toad (Reptile)

The horned toad is a flat-bodied lizard that lives up to its name; it has spines along its back and sides and horns on its head. The female horned toad lays clutches of six to ten eggs. A desert dweller, it remains active even when the temperature is 38°C (100°F). It lives among the sand and rocks and feeds on insects and spiders. It is a brown lizard, 5-17 cm (2-7 in) long.

Collared Lizard (Reptile)

The collared lizard is a large, bright green lizard 20-35 cm (8-14 in) long. Its home is in the desert area where there are few plants. It sports a black and white collar with white spots on its body. The female lizard lays three to eight eggs in midsummer. Its favorite foods are insects and spiders.

Desert Tortoise (Reptile)

Lumbering across the desert sands, the desert tortoise searches for flowers or leaves to eat from the succulent vegetation. The 25-35 cm (10-14 in) desert tortoise is protected from the drying effects of the extreme heat and predators by its thick shell. The tortoise has flat front feet with legs that have large scales; the hind legs and feet are round and stumpy. During the hot and cold seasons, it retreats to its burrow and sleeps until the weather becomes more favorable. The female tortoise digs a nest in the sand where it lays two to three clutches of 2-14 hard round eggs.

Living Things of the Desert

	Tarantula (Spider) The tarantula is a large, hairy spider that lives in the desert area. It is often seen crossing the road after sunset or near dawn. It eats insects, lizards, and other small animals. The tarantula is gray to dark brown in color and 5-6 cm (2-2.5 in) in size. The female tarantula can lay hundreds of eggs in an egg case. She lives up to 20 years.
	Tarantula Hawk (Insect) The tarantula hawk is a velvety black wasp that hunts for a spider that is three times its size. The tarantula hawk is an insect that is only 12-20 mm (0.5-0.75 in) in length, but it is able to kill a tarantula to feed its babies. The female wasp stings the tarantula to paralyze it, drags it to a burrow, and lays her eggs on it. The wasp's larvae feed on the spider. The adult wasp drinks nectar.
	Ants (Insect) Ants are very familiar insects that are mostly black, brown, or reddish in color. Ants live in colonies underground or in tunnels hollowed out in dead wood. Most ants eat dead insects or animals for food.
	Scorpion (Invertebrate) This desert creature roams the sands at night in search of its prey. It has two pincers on the front of its body and a long tail that curves upward. The scorpion uses the stinger on the end of its tail to kill spiders and large insects for food and for self-defense. The desert scorpion measures 14 cm (5.5 in) in length, has a light brown body with yellow legs and tail. It does not normally sting humans unless provoked. Owls and bats, which hunt at night, find the scorpion a tasty meal.
	Road Runner (Bird) The road runner received its name by its habit of running ahead of slow-moving vehicles. The road runner has long sturdy legs and leaves a distinctive X-shaped track in the sand. Its strong beak acts as a small sword to stab its prey. It eats a varied diet of small birds, scorpions, lizards, snakes, seeds, and fruits. The road runner is a large bird, measuring 60 cm (2 ft) in length including the tail. The female lays three to five white eggs in a shallow basket-shaped nest. Today it is one of the most recognized and welcomed of the desert birds.
	Elf Owl (Bird) The smallest of the owls, only 13-15 cm (5-6 in) tall, the elf owl lives almost exclusively on large insects of the desert. It hunts at night and can be located by its high-pitched call. The elf owl nests in a hole in the saguaro cactus where it lays three to four white eggs. It has gray-brown feathers, big yellow eyes, and a short tail.

Living Things of the Desert

	Gambel's Quail (Bird) Living in the desert thickets and cactus scrub, the gambel's quail lives in large family groups of 30-40 birds. A large grayish bird, 25-29 cm (10-11 in) in length, it has brown wings and a red cap with a teardrop-shaped head plume. The gambel's quail lives on seeds and small insects. It makes its nest on the ground in small depressions where it lays 10-20 eggs.
	Gila Woodpecker (Bird) The gila woodpecker is 20-25 cm (8-10 in) long. Its back is black and white while its head and body are a light tan. The cap of its head is a red color. The gila woodpecker hunts for insects in the brushy areas and open desert areas of the saguaro cactus. It drills a hole in the saguaro cactus to make a nest where it lays three to five white eggs. Many other birds and animals later use these holes for their nests.
	Red-Tailed Hawk (Bird) A large bird that spends much time soaring in the air, the red-tailed hawk likes open areas where it is easy to spot its prey. It has an important role in controlling rats, lizards, and squirrels. It is a dark brown bird with a rusty red tail. The red-tailed hawk measures 62 cm (25 in) in length. The female makes her nest on a cliff or in a tree where she lays one to four eggs.

Living Things of the Desert

Living Things	Home	Food	Characteristics
Birds			
Elf Owl	Nests in abandoned woodpecker holes in cactus	Rodents	Large eyes; talons; sharp beak; fluffy feathers for silent flying; 13-15 cm (5-6 in)
Gila Woodpecker	Drills holes in saguaro cactus for nest	Insects	Long sharp bill; strong neck muscles; sharp claws; 20-25 cm (8-10 in)
Road Runner	Nests in low shrubs or cactus groups	Insects, mice, snakes, lizards	Runs 25 km/h (15 mph); sharp claws; large heavy beak; 60 cm (2 ft)
Gambel's Quail	Nests on ground in shrubs	Seeds	Lives in families; scatters when alarmed; 25-29 cm (10-11 in)
Red-Tailed Hawk	Nests in trees (mesquite, cottonwood)	Small mammals, birds, snakes	Sharp, curved talons and beak; sharp eyes; 60-65 cm (25 in)
Reptiles			
Sidewinder	Under small rocks	Small rodents	Has scales; rattles on tail; poisonous; moves in a sideways fashion; 45 cm (18 in)
Collared Lizard	Rocks	Insects, spiders	Tail used for defense; 20-35 cm (8-14 in)
Horned Toad	Rocks, sand	Insects, spiders	Lizard; horns; has scales; flattened body; spines; 5-17 cm (2-7 in)
Desert Tortoise	Underground, rocks	Plants	Lays eggs in sand; has shell; has scales; lives to 100 years; beak to cut food; 25-35 cm (10-14 in)
Gila Monster	Under rocks, in burrows	Birds, reptiles, some vegetation, eggs, rodents	Poisonous; has scales; heavy body; stores fat in tail; 45 cm (18 in)

Living Things of the Desert

Living Things	Home	Food	Characteristics
Mammals			
Jack Rabbit	Under rocks, not in burrows	Plants	Not a hare; blood vessels in large ears cool body; fast runner; 60 cm (2 ft)
Long-Nosed Bat	In crevasses and caves	Cactus flower nectar	Hangs from high places; pollinates flowers; 30 cm (12 in) wingspan; 30 g (1 oz)
Coyote	Den dug under rocks	Rabbits, mice, insects, reptiles	Fast; sharp teeth; hunts at night; 60 cm (2 ft) tall, 1.2 m (4 ft) long;
Kangaroo Rat	Underground burrows	Seeds, grasses	Can live without water, gets moisture from seeds and plants; feeds at night; can leap long distances; 10-12 cm (4-4.5 in)
Pocket Mouse	Underground burrows	Seeds	Carries seeds in cheek pouch; active at night; 11-13 cm (4-5 in)
Insects			
Tarantula Hawk		Tarantulas	Large blue, red, and green wasp; paralyzes tarantula with venom to provide live food for brood
Ants	Underground tunnels	Dead insects	Black, brown; predators; scavengers; 1-25 mm (0.06-1 in)
Spider			
Tarantula	Under rocks, in ground	Insects	Large, hairy, brown/black body; 5-6 cm (2-2.5 in)
Invertebrate			
Scorpion	In crevices, under rocks, in litter	Insects, spiders	Long, segmented tail; poisonous sting in tail; active at night; body 14 cm (5.5 in)

Living Things of the Desert

Living Things	Color	Size	Characteristics
Plants			
Ocotillo	Gray-green	15-65 cm (6-25 in) tall	Spiny stems grow like switches; grow leaves and scarlet flowers after rain; dry, thorny sticks during dry season
Saguaro	Brownish-green, greenish-white flowers	18 m (60 ft) tall; can weigh 9070 kg (10 T)	Largest cactus in US; state flower of Arizona; bats, birds, and insects gather nectar from blossoms
Prickly-Pear Cactus	Gray-green	60 cm (2 ft)	Pear-shaped fruit, good to eat; plant protected with 5 cm (2 in) spines
Barrel Cactus	Dark green	3 m (10 ft)	A rounded barrel shape; absorbs water in winter
Sagebrush	Gray-green	60-150 cm (2-5 ft)	Bushy; small leaves; bitter taste; yellow or white flowers
Strawberry Hedge-hog Cactus	Green	2.5-30 cm (1-12 in)	Upright stems; showy red flowers; spines in clusters
Beavertail Cactus	Grayish-green with pink flowers	5-30 cm (2-12 in)	Flat, beavertail-shaped stems, pink flowers
Soapweed	Greenish-white to pinkish flowers	60-300 cm (2-10 ft)	Native Americans used bulb for soap, roasted bulb used for glue and medicine

123

Mountains

Mountains have always attracted people for many reasons — economic (mining, lumbering, recreation), scientific (geology, meteorology, biology), aesthetics (just for the beauty of the area), and adventure (hiking, skiing, backpacking).

A mountain is a large region of land that projects above its surrounding area. It is a major feature of the surrounding area. Hills do not rise as high above the environment as mountains. But most mountains will, in time, be worn down into hills. Most mountains are part of a mountain range, such as the Rocky Mountains, Appalachian Mountains, and the Sierra Nevada Mountains. Mount Everest is the highest mountain on the land part of Earth, but it is not the highest mountain. Mauna Kea is considered the tallest mountain if it is measured from its island peak to its base on the bottom of the ocean.

Mountains have been formed by several methods: the movement of the continental plates of the Earth create folded mountains along their edges where they have been forced into each other; undersea mountains form where two plates are pulled apart and hot molten rock seeps through from the interior of the Earth; volcanic mountains rise along the edges of the plates where one crust is plunging beneath another and in areas where there is a weak spot in the crust and magma seeps through.

Several factors affect the weather and climate on mountains. The higher you climb, the colder it gets. This is because the air becomes thinner and cannot hold as much heat as at sea level. There is also less oxygen in the air at the higher elevations. The mountains are often very windy places because there is little to shelter them from the winds, especially on the higher slopes. Cold air at the high elevations is heavy, so it tends to slide down the mountainsides creating strong winds. The amount of rain falling on a mountainside depends on the direction of the prevailing winds. When air is forced to rise to get over the mountains, it loses moisture. Moisture falls from the clouds, making one side green and lush and the other side more desertlike.

Because many mountains are so high in elevation, they provide several different levels, or zones, for plant and animal life. The lower zones of the mountains tend to have many different kinds of deciduous trees such as maples, oaks, and chestnuts along with shrubs, grasses, and many wildflowers. Many varieties of animals, both large and small, can be found in the warmer, lower areas. As you climb higher on the mountain, the temperatures become colder and the trees become the needle-like evergreens such as spruce, fir, and pine; plants are smaller and there are fewer animals. The tallest mountains have heights that are above the tree line. The only plants that can withstand the cold and the wind are small twisted shrubs and plants growing in the protected areas and mosses and lichen that grow on the rocks.

The wildlife is an important part of the mountain habitat and has in many cases made adaptations to live in this area. The larger species of wildlife are abundant in the forests of the mountains. Bears, wildcats, deer, elk, and mountain sheep are some of the animals living here. Evidences of smaller mammals can also be found. Squirrels are plentiful, porcupines, martens, and marmots occupy an important part in the ecology of the area. The high elevations are especially rich in bird life, with such species as the spotted owl, red-tailed hawk, Clark's nutcracker, woodpeckers, Stellar jay, tanager, and bald eagle living here.

Mountains affect the whole area surrounding them: climate, transportation, commerce, agriculture, and recreation.

Mountains

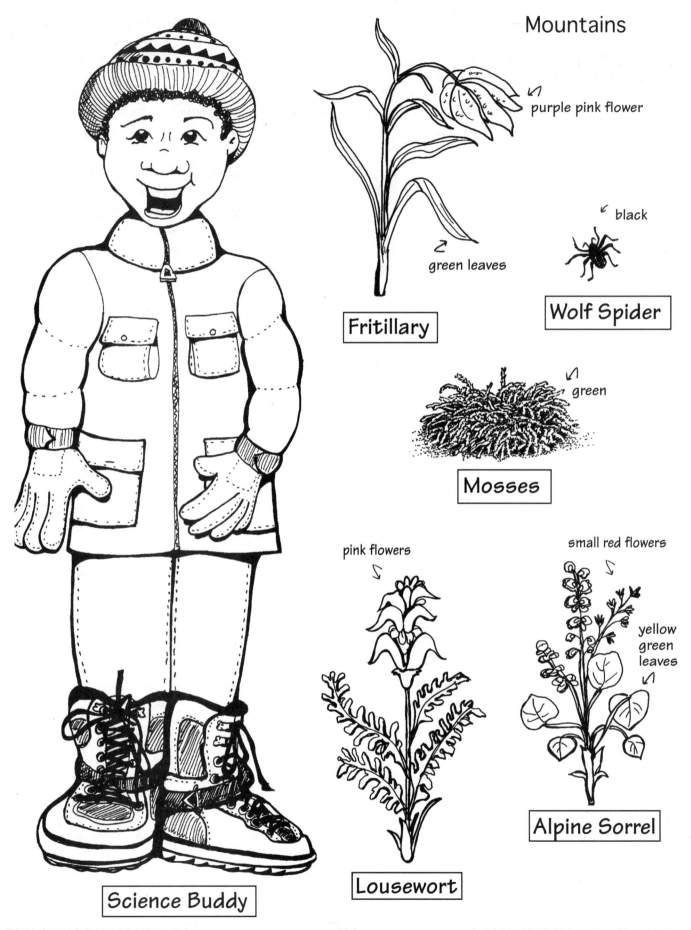

purple pink flower

green leaves

Fritillary

black

Wolf Spider

green

Mosses

pink flowers

Lousewort

small red flowers

yellow green leaves

Alpine Sorrel

Science Buddy

126

Mountains

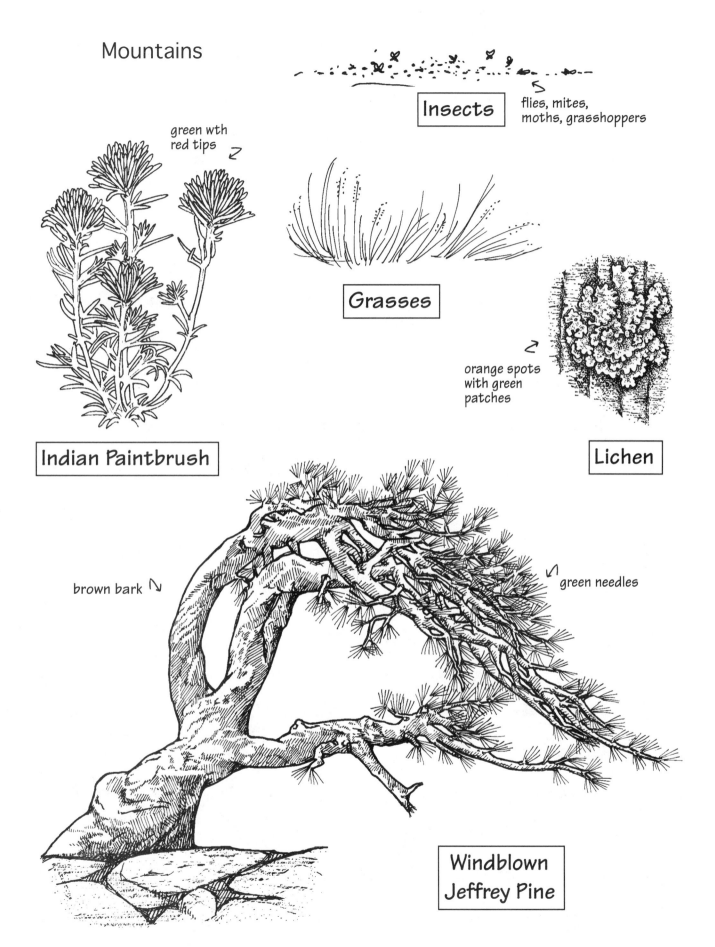

Insects — flies, mites, moths, grasshoppers

green wth red tips

Grasses

orange spots with green patches

Indian Paintbrush

Lichen

brown bark

green needles

Windblown Jeffrey Pine

Mountains

golden brown with white-tipped hairs

brown and white back

White-Tailed Ptarmigan

Grizzly Bear

white with yellow tinge

golden brown

Golden Eagle

Mountain Goat

Mountains

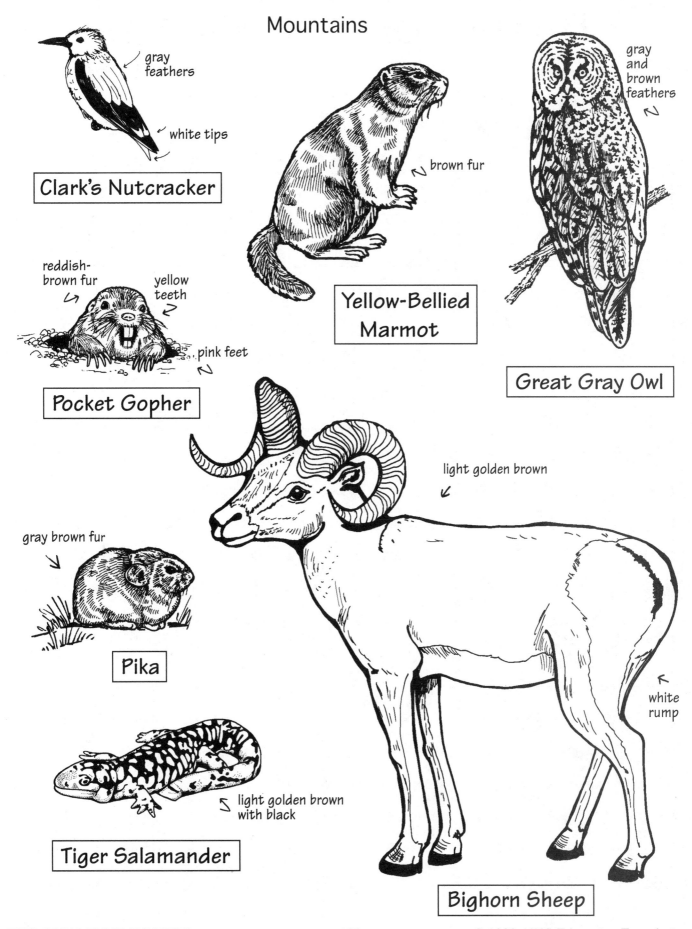

gray feathers

white tips

Clark's Nutcracker

brown fur

Yellow-Bellied Marmot

gray and brown feathers

Great Gray Owl

reddish-brown fur

yellow teeth

pink feet

Pocket Gopher

light golden brown

gray brown fur

Pika

white rump

light golden brown with black

Tiger Salamander

Bighorn Sheep

Living Things of the Mountains

Grizzly Bear   (Mammal)

As one of the largest omnivore animals, the grizzly bear eats everything from beetle grubs and acorns to small mammals. The grizzly bear takes its name from the long, silver-tipped hairs on its back and shoulders which give its coat a grizzled appearance. Most of these bears spend the winter months asleep. It is during this time that the female bear gives birth to her two cubs. The largest of the three North American bears, the grizzly is 180-220 cm (6-7 ft) long and weighs 300-400 kg (600-800 lbs). In its natural home the grizzly has no enemies or predators. It has small eyes and ears but a very keen sense of smell. It has an expected lifespan of 30 years.

Bighorn Sheep   (Mammal)

A very elusive animal, the bighorn sheep has big heavy horns, which are often used as battering rams during the mating season. The heavy horns of the male, can weigh up to 14 kg (30 lbs) and curl in a C-shape. The bighorn sheep is a light brown colored animal with a white underside and rump. It is 168 cm (5.5 ft) long and weighs 115-130 kg (250-280 lb). Although it is heavy-bodied, the mountain sheep has a remarkable ability to climb and jump on the rugged, sparsely-wooded mountain slopes that are inaccessible to most large animals. The pads on its feet help the mountain sheep grip rocks and climb the cliffs. It feeds on grassy vegetation and shrubby plants. The female usually gives birth to one lamb, but she will occasionally bear twins. The mountain sheep is preyed upon by mountain lions and eagles. Its lifespan is 15-20 years.

Mountain Goat   (Mammal)

A sure-footed animal of the highland region, the mountain goat can be found on steep slopes and cliffs above the timberline. This animal's compact body and short legs help it climb in the rugged mountainous areas. White fur and short black horns that curve backward are characteristic of this animal. It grazes on grasses, sedges, and shrubs of the highlands. It grows to a length of 150 cm (5 ft) and 100 cm (3.5 ft) shoulder height, weighing 75 to 130 kg (160-280 lbs). The female mountain goat usually has one kid. The goat can live up to 18 years.

Yellow-Bellied Marmot   (Mammal)

This fat little animal can be seen peering at intruders from a large boulder near its home. It gives a shrill, sharp whistle when alarmed. The brown, furry marmot can be found on rocky slopes in the high mountains, often sunbathing on top of large rocks. It feeds on spiders and worms and on the grasses and shrubs of the alpine meadows during the summers. During the fall and winter, it hibernates in subterranean nests. The female marmot will have her young, averaging three babies, in this burrow. The babies are born blind and helpless, but they mature rapidly. An adult marmot weighs 5.4 kg (12 lbs) or more and is up to 43 cm (17 in) long with a bushy 18 cm (7 in) tail.

Living Things of the Mountains

Pika   (Mammal)

One of the busiest animals above the timberline is the pika. This small ball of fur harvests a variety of plants during the short mountain summer. It cuts grasses and plants and stacks the "hay" in piles to cure for its winter food. The pika lives in a loose rocky area on the mountainside where it can hide in crevices. It is active under the snow all winter long. A small gray brown creature measuring 18-20 cm (7-8 in) long, it has short, broad, rounded ears. The female pika will have a litter of 3-13 young in the spring. The pika can have a lifespan of six years.

Pocket Gopher   (Mammal)

The pocket gopher is an animal that is built for digging. It has legs that are stubby and muscular. Its feet are powerful with long claws to help with the burrowing. A reddish-brown fur covers a 70-90 g (3-3.5 oz) body, 18-20 cm (7-8 in) long. The gopher's large yellow teeth protrude so that it can keep dirt from entering its mouth during underground digging. The "pockets," extending from cheek to shoulder that give it its name, are often crammed with food or bedding material for nests. In this nest the five young are born and stay for about 100 days. The burrowing done by gophers is good for the soil. It allows air and water into the soil thereby helping to conserve groundwater and to prevent erosion. The pocket gopher is a vegetarian, eating only roots, tubers, and soft-stemmed plants. It is hunted by gophers, snakes, and owls.

Great Gray Owl   (Bird)

The largest owl in the United States, the great gray owl has a large head, large eyes, and hooked bill. It is brownish-gray bird with a large face that has concentric gray and brown circles around yellow eyes. It feeds on small mammals and birds. The great gray owl is about 70 cm (27 in) tall. It has a remarkably small body within a large mass of feathers that provides excellent insulation against the cold. It nests in an abandoned hawk's or crow's nest in a tall tree where two to five eggs are laid.

Clark's Nutcracker   (Bird)

The Clark's nutcracker is a large bird that can be found in the forests near the tree line. It is light gray bird with a white face and a long, sharply-pointed bill and long tail. It looks like a combination of a woodpecker and a crow. It eats the nuts from the pine trees and insects. It is 30 cm (12 in) long. The nutcracker builds its nest of sticks in a coniferous tree where two to six green spotted eggs are laid.

White-Tailed Ptarmigan   (Bird)

The white-tailed ptarmigan is a hardy bird that lives in the high mountain area and seldom descends to the tree line. Its feathered feet help it to conserve heat. The ptarmigan has a mottled brown back and white tail, belly, and wings. In the winter this bird turns all white in color. The ptarmigan hides in a snow bank for protection in the winter. It feeds on seeds and grains in summer; in the winter it eats willow buds. The white-tailed ptarmigan measures 30 cm (12 in) in length. The female ptarmigan lays six to eight buff-colored eggs in a shallow depression lined with grasses and feathers.

Living Things of the Mountains

Golden Eagle (Bird)

One of the largest of the raptors in the mountain areas, the golden eagle is a magnificent flier and a fierce hunter. It soars in the air with its huge, broad wings looking for rabbits, squirrels, and rodents. A brown bird with golden head and neck, it is about 1 m (39 in) in length with a 2 m (7 ft) wingspan. It builds a stick nest on a rock ledge in which to lays its two white eggs and raise its young. The golden eagle can live 15-20 years.

Tiger Salamander (Amphibian)

The tiger salamander is the world's largest land-dwelling salamander. It has a stout body with a broad head and small eyes. The tiger salamander is found in widespread areas. Its colors are variable, quite often large light spots on a dark background. It is one of the few salamanders that can be found at 3000 m (11,000 ft) elevations. The tiger salamander lives beneath debris and eats insects and small rodents. It grows to 40 cm (15 in) in length.

Insects (Insects)

The high mountains do not make very welcome homes for insects. Those insects that are there are usually either migrating or are blown by the winds into the high country. The cold temperatures restrict their activity so they are very slow moving. In the mountains most insects fly and crawl about during the daytime when they can be warmed by the sunshine. At night they take shelter in the warm ground or in rock cracks and crevices. Because of the scarce food supply of plants, animal blood, and pollen, and the cold temperatures, many of the winged insects — mites, grasshoppers, flies, moths — take longer to develop.

Wolf Spider (Spider)

The wolf spider is known as a hunter. It hunts down and catches its prey with the help of its acute eyesight — it has eight eyes in three rows. The wolf spider lives in burrows in the ground and hunts at night. It does not spin a web. Its eight long legs have small claws at the end. The wolf spider's dark color conceals it in the leaves and rocks. This 2.5 cm (1 in) long spider eats mostly insects, but occasionally will eat other spiders.

Lichen (Plant)

Lichens seem like ordinary plants, but they are composed of two separate plants — a fungus and an algae — living in close association. Lichens grow as thin, flat crusts on rocks, trees, and bare soil. They help to break down the rock and create pockets of soil where seeds of other plants can gain a foothold. Usually only a few inches in diameter, many of them are brightly colored red, orange, yellow, and green. Besides helping to form soil, lichens have another place in nature — they serve as food for snails and insects. Humans use them to produce dyes. They are a source of litmus, the dye used in chemical tests for acidity.

Living Things of the Mountains

	**Mosses** **(Plant)** Mosses are generally small plants, growing only a few inches high or creeping flat across the rocks and ground. They are quite tough and hardy and can grow in the harsh conditions of the higher elevations of the mountains. The roots of mosses help by breaking down the rocks and forming soil in which other plants can grow. Mosses also protect barren soil from erosion.
	**Jeffrey Pine** **(Tree)** Many of the bushes or trees, such as the Jeffrey pine, that grow on the open slopes of the high mountains are stunted and shaped by the winds and harsh weather conditions. The conifer trees that do survive have been dwarfed, twisted, and misshapen by the relentless winds and heavy snowpacks. Sometimes these trees are called "banner trees." They show flagging, in which all the branches grow on the side of the plant away from the prevailing winds. But they are survivors and provide shelter for many of the small inhabitants of the region.
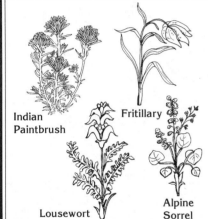

Indian Paintbrush   Fritillary

Lousewort   Alpine Sorrel | **Mountain Wildflowers**   **(Flowers)**
    Flowers bloom during the short summer days in the high mountains. These alpine areas have little rainfall, high winds, and little soil so the plants must adapt to their surroundings. Many alpine plants grow on the leeward side of rocks or other obstructions which help to keep them warm and moist. Their small size and narrow leaves help to store water and reduce exposure to the strong sunlight. The plants will flower shortly after the snow melts which allows time for their seeds to be dispersed and start to establish themselves before the next winter starts. One unusual feature of these plants is the large showy flowers which attracts pollinating insects. Some examples of the wildflowers that can grow in the mountains are the **alpine sorrel**, **lousewort**, **fritillary**, and **Indian paintbrush**. |

Living Things of the Mountains

Living Things	Home	Food	Characteristics
Mammals			
Grizzly Bear	Forest, mountains	Berries, small animals, insects, dead animals, fish	Golden brown in color; hump above shoulders; hibernate in winter; 180-220 cm (6-7 ft) long; 130 cm (4.25 ft) tall at shoulder; 300-400 kg (600-800 lbs)
Bighorn Sheep	High mountains, rugged cliffs	Grasses, shrubs	Brown body, white rump; good climber; heavy, curved horns; 168 cm (5.5 ft); 115-130 kg (250-280 lbs)
Mountains Goats	Steep mountain slopes and cliffs	Grasses, shrubs, sedges	White fur; short black horns; short legs; flexible hoofs for climbing; 150 cm (5 ft)
Yellow-Bellied Marmot	Rocky slopes of mountains	Grasses, shrubs	Brown, furry animal; hibernates in winter; 43 cm (17 in)
Pika	Mountains, above tree line	Grasses	Small gray brown animal; harvests and dries grasses for winter use; no tail; 18-20 cm (7 -8 in)
Pocket Gopher	Meadow, soft soil	Roots, leafy vegetation, tubers	Reddish-brown; large yellow teeth; long claws; cheek pockets; 13-22 cm (5-9 in)
Birds			
Golden Eagle	Mountain areas	Rabbits, rodents, squirrels	Huge, soaring bird; good flier; fast hunter; brown with golden crown and neck; 1 m (39 in) long; 2 m (7 ft) wingspan
White-Tailed Ptarmigan	Mountains about tree line	Seeds, willow bud	Mottled brown bird; white tail, belly, and wings; all white in winter; feathered feet; 30 cm (1 ft) in length

Living Things of the Mountains

Living Things	Home	Food	Characteristics
Great Gray Owl	Forest trees, mountain meadows	Rodents, small mammals	Large owl; yellow eyes; hooked bill; brownish-gray; 70 cm (27 in)
Clark's Nutcracker	Forests, open areas	Pine nuts, insects	Gray bird; white face; long tail; long bill; 30 cm (1 ft)
Amphibian			
Tiger Salamander	Moist areas	Insects, rodents	Large, stout body; dark color with light background; 40 cm (15 in)
Spiders and Insects			
Wolf Spider	Sandy areas	Insects	Dark spider; eight eyes; does not spin a web; 25 mm (1 in)
Insects	Cracks in rock, on ground	Plants, animal blood, pollen	Flies; moths; mites; grasshoppers; fly and crawl around in daytime to be warmed
Plants			
Jeffrey Pine Tree	Open slopes		Trees are stunted and twisted by wind; often called "banner tree"; branches grow on one side of tree
Mosses	On ground and rocks		Small green plants; help protect soil from erosion; breaks down rocks
Lichen	Rocks, trees, ground		Plant composed of algae and fungus; bright colors; helps break down rock into soil

Ocean

Oceans

Our planet, as seen from outer space, is a beautiful blue color. This distinctive coloration comes from the vast ocean that covers more than 70% of the Earth's surface. Ours is a watery planet unlike any other in the solar system. The ocean contains almost all the water on Earth.

The waters of the ocean form one great connected body; however, the continents divide this great body of water into four major parts. They are, in order of size from largest to smallest, the Pacific Ocean, the Atlantic Ocean, the Indian Ocean, and the Arctic Ocean.

The ocean acts as a great heat reservoir, moderating the high and low temperatures of the seasons. During the summer, the water is cooler than the surrounding land areas. Breezes flowing over the water onto the land cool the land. During the winter, the water retains some of the heat it gained in the summer and it warms the land near it.

Oceans play a major role in determining the climates of the Earth. The water holds a large amount of heat and the currents of the oceans move it around. The large currents, like the Gulf Stream, play an important role in climate by moving warm or cool water from one place to another. Ocean temperatures also help determine the locations of large high and low pressure areas.

The ocean is teeming with living things which provide food for sea life and humans and other animals on land. The ocean supports life from the very small to the very large. The food chain in the sea has its base in plankton, tiny plant and animal organisms that drift in enormous numbers throughout the ocean. Phytoplankton (plant) and zooplankton (animal) are important primary elements in the ocean's food chain. The phytoplankton turn the sun's energy into food. The zooplankton feed on these microscopic plants. Krill, a small shrimp-like crustacean, is the most numerous species. It provides the major link in the transfer of energy from the plankton to the larger fish.

Sponges, coral, shrimp, sea horses, and scallops are a few of the smaller sea animals that depend on phytoplankton for their food. The large baleen whales, such as the humpback, gulp large amounts of krill, shrimp, and small fish from the sea.

Large fish feed on smaller sea animals such as shrimp, scallops, squid, and crabs. The fish in turn become food for the still larger sea animals like the dolphins, sharks, and seals.

Coral reefs in the warm waters of the western Pacific Ocean provide shelter for a multitude of marine animals, more than almost any other habitat on Earth. Coral is an animal that actually makes rock by taking the salts and minerals from the water, combining them, and secreting calcium-carbonate (limestone).

Coral is very sensitive to temperature changes and pollution, but it can withstand hurricanes. Coral does not move but has tentacles that catch plankton for food. It reproduces, communicates, and builds reefs. A coral reef takes thousands of years to form. It is built of the skeletons of the coral. The coral look like white rock during the day, but at night, when they come out to feed, they are very colorful. Australia's Great Barrier Reef is perhaps the largest and best known of all the coral reefs in the world.

The fan coral and the staghorn coral are but two of the thousands of different coral that inhabit the warmer oceans of the world. Many sea creatures live in and around the coral reefs. The shy octopus is rarely seen; it hides in cracks and crevices of the coral reef, but can move by jet siphon with astonishing speed. The parrotfish is a resident that feeds by scraping algae off the coral. With its parrot-shaped beak and sharp teeth, it bites through the coral to get at the algae, thereby reducing the coral to white sand. The moray eel hides in small crevices, but can move fast to catch its food. The clownfish has a unique relationship with the sea anemone of the reef. The sea anemone is a fish eater, yet the clownfish is able to hide among the anemone's poisonous waving tentacles. To do this, the clownfish secretes a slimy substance that protects it from the anemone's sting. When a predator fish chases the clownfish, the clownfish hides in the tentacles of the sea anemone and the sea anemone ends up getting to feast on the predator. The coral reef borders on water deep enough that sharks, dolphins, and whales are nearby feeding on the many creatures found there.

Abundant life in the ocean depends on the nutrients available in the water. Perhaps the most productive surface water is in the northern and southern parts of the oceans where the cold water rises from the depths carrying large amounts of minerals. Currents carry this rich water from the cold areas toward the warmer climates where the inhabitants of the coral reefs can benefit from the nutrients.

Ocean

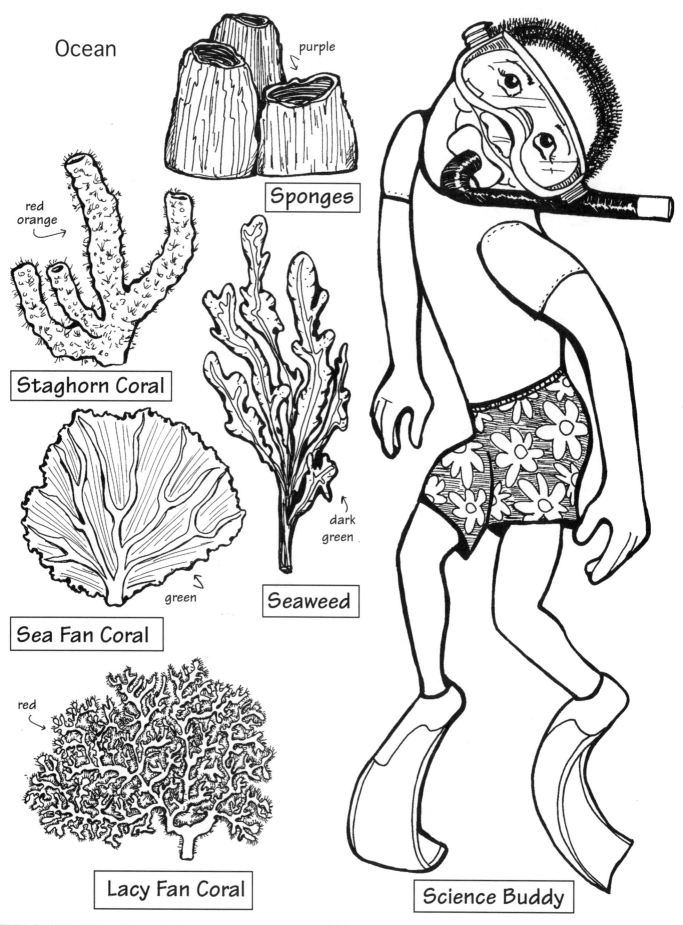

purple

Sponges

red orange

Staghorn Coral

Sea Fan Coral

green

Seaweed

dark green

Lacy Fan Coral

red

Science Buddy

Ocean

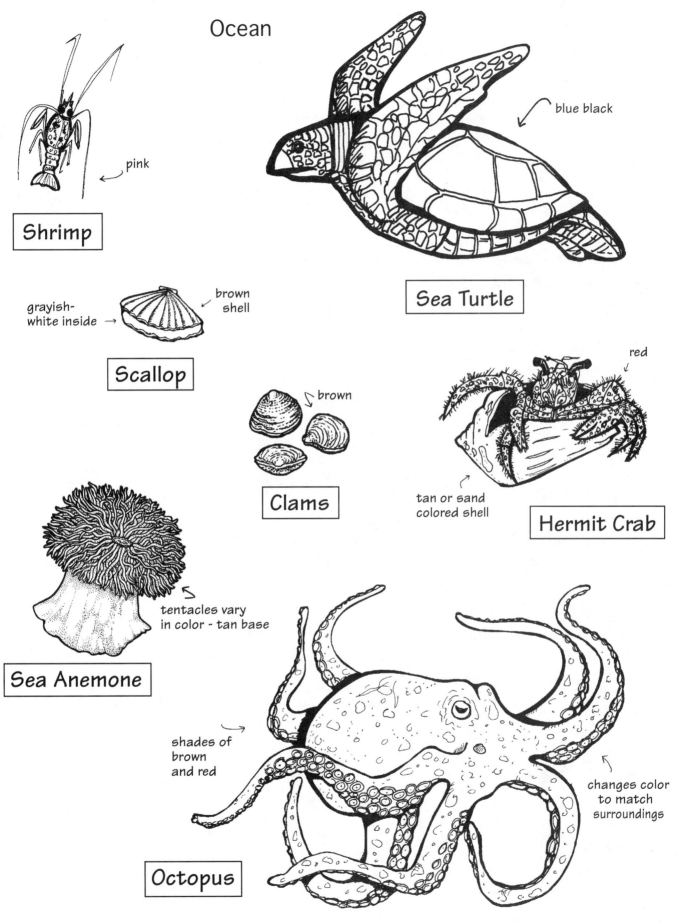

pink

Shrimp

blue black

Sea Turtle

grayish-white inside →   brown shell

Scallop

↱ brown

Clams

red

tan or sand colored shell

Hermit Crab

tentacles vary in color - tan base

Sea Anemone

shades of brown and red

changes color to match surroundings

Octopus

Ocean

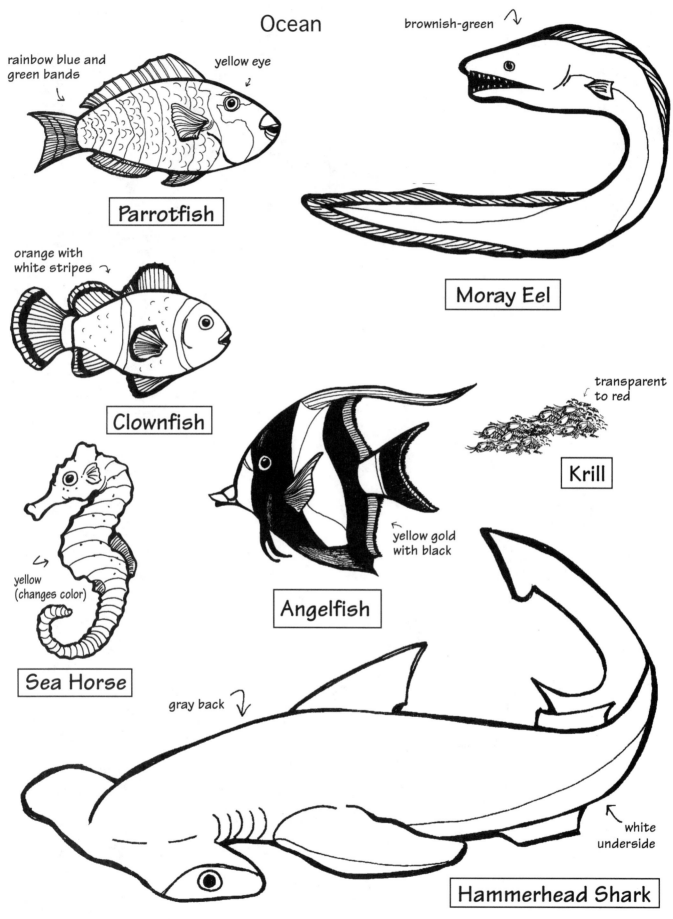

brownish-green

rainbow blue and
green bands

yellow eye

Parrotfish

Moray Eel

orange with
white stripes

Clownfish

transparent
to red

Krill

yellow gold
with black

Angelfish

yellow
(changes color)

Sea Horse

gray back

white
underside

Hammerhead Shark

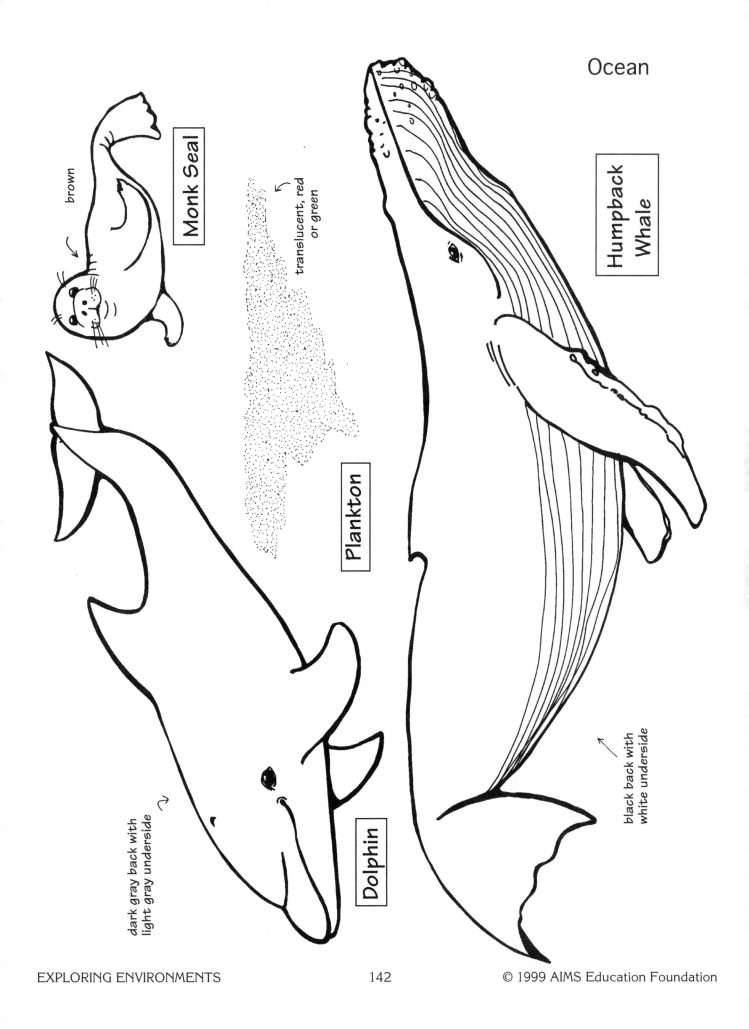

Ocean

Monk Seal

brown

Humpback
Whale

translucent, red
or green

Plankton

black back with
white underside

dark gray back with
light gray underside

Dolphin

Living Things of the Oceans

Sea Turtle   (Reptile)

The leatherback turtle is unusual because it has a leathery covering over its shell instead of the usual horny shield of most turtles. It swims alone except during the breeding season. The leatherback turtle is the largest of all living turtles and can live 40-50 years. This sea turtle can grow up to 2 m (6 ft) in length and weigh 273-727 kg (600-1,600 lb). It is a gray to blue black color. It has winglike, tapering flippers that may span 4 m (11 ft). It swims by beating its very powerful foreflippers like a bird flaps its wings. The female sea turtle only comes ashore to lay eggs. She digs a deep hole in the sand and lays more than 100 golfball-sized eggs, covers them with sand and heads out to sea. The eggs hatch about eight weeks later and the little hatchlings find their own way to the sea. The babies eat fish, algae, crabs, and shrimp. The adults, since they cannot swim fast enough to catch fish and squid, eat jellyfish and plankton that drift with the currents. They also feed on other mollusks and crustaceans.

Clam   (Mollusk)

The clam is a mollusk with a shell that has two parts, or valves. The shells are often oval in shape with a brown coating and a white interior. The clam usually lives in the sand just below the low tide line. It is a filter feeder; it draws in seawater and filters out tiny food particles. Many people consider the clam a delicious seafood.

Scallop   (Mollusk)

The scallop, a delicacy for both humans and other sea life, has a beautiful shell. The outside of the shell is usually a mottled brown, but inside the shell is a grayish-white to white color. The scallop moves in a zigzag motion through the water by snapping its valves open and shut. Tentacles that protrude between the shells help it feel for food. It averages in size from 5-15 cm (2-6 in). A scallop can usually be found attached to a rock, or a piling, or buried in mud at the bottom of the bay.

Octopus   (Mollusk)

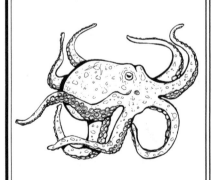

The octopus is a sea creature with an oval body and eight arms. These arms feel and taste things and are also used for walking. Suction disks that hold fish and other prey are found on each arm. An octopus can swim but usually will crawl, using its suckers to hold on to rocks. The octopus swims by squeezing a jet of water out through the back of its body much like jet propulsion. An octopus is a rather shy creature that can often be found among the rocks or coral reef where it hides. As a protection, this creature can change color to match its surroundings but it is most often a red or brown color. A small octopus that occupies a rock pool may not grow over 30 cm (1 ft) in size, while one that lives in the open water can grow much larger — even up to 3 m (10 ft). The octopus is one of the few sea animals that has neither a hard shell nor a backbone.

Living Things of the Oceans

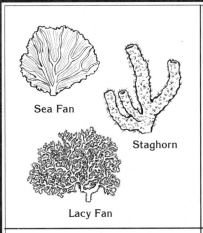

Sea Fan

Staghorn

Lacy Fan

Coral   (Invertebrate)

Coral is an interesting animal that looks like a rock, sometimes acts like a plant, and shoots darts to capture plankton. A coral polyp has a soft body which lives in a cup-shaped shelter. During the day it hides, but at night it sends out tentacles from its shelter to gather food. Coral comes in all different sizes, shapes, and colors. The **staghorn coral** (looks like a deer's horn), **sea fan coral** (resembles a ladies fan), and **lacy fan coral** (like a dainty piece of lace) are just a few of the hundreds of kinds of coral found in the ocean. The coral reef, a line or ridge of coral, offers a place of protection for many kinds of fish, but it is also attacked by other inhabitants such as sea stars, parrotfish, shrimp. The coral need clean, warm tropical water that is shallow enough for sunlight to reach them.

Sea Anemone   (Invertebrate)

The sea anemone is a soft animal that has a body shaped like a column that is topped with many feathery-looking tentacles. The tentacles have special stinging cells that poison their prey. The prey is then pulled toward the anemone's mouth where more stings will kill the animal. Only the clownfish seems to be able to live with the anemone without becoming the anemone's dinner. The sea anemone is 5-10 cm (2-4 in) tall and lives on rocks and pilings near the shore.

Sponges   (Invertebrate)

Scientists originally thought sponges were plants, but later found them to be animals. In order to gather food, sponges draw water in through small openings in their bodies. Once the food particles are filtered out, the water then exits from their bodies through larger holes. An average-sized sponge draws about 170 liters (45 gal) of water through its system in a single day! Sponges come in many shapes: some look like trees, others look like gloves, cups, or domes. They range greatly in size, from as small as a pinhead to 2.5 m (8 ft) in diameter. Sponges also vary in color: white, gray, yellow, orange, red, green, blue, purple, or black. The dried bodies of some sponges are used in our homes as cleaning tools.

Shrimp   (Invertebrate)

Shrimp, a popular shellfish food eaten in the United States, are small crustaceans found in sea water in most parts of the world. They come in many different sizes from the small fairy shrimp to the large edible prawns. They range in size from 2.5-30 cm (1-12 in) long. Shrimp eat plankton and dead plants and animals. They, in turn, are eaten by larger fish. Shrimp come in many different colors, most often with a gray, white, or pink body. The shrimp's external skeleton is hard and surrounds the body. As it grows it sheds its skeleton many times and grows new ones.

Living Things of the Oceans

	**Hermit Crab** (Invertebrate) The hermit crab is a small crab that lives in tide pools. It is about 3-4 cm (1-1.5 in) long. It has a soft body so it must find a shelter where it can be protected. The hermit crab lives in shells abandoned by other animals, quite often those of snails. You can see it carrying its shell wherever it goes. As it outgrows its present shell, it must find a larger shell to keep pace with its growth. A hermit crab sifts through the mud to find small plants and animals to eat. The moray eel considers the hermit crab one of the main items on its menu.
	**Moray Eel** (Fish) Moray eels hide in coral reefs during the day and venture out after dark to feed. They are fierce-looking creatures with long slender bodies — 30-120 cm (1-4 ft) — and mouths filled with sharp teeth. There is a a single long, continuous fin that runs the length of their bodies. They are not poisonous, but can inflict painful bites on any hand that is thrust into their holes. Since eels hunt for food only at night, they use their sense of smell to find their food. Small fish, octopus, and squid provide the main part of the eel's diet.
	**Sea Horse** (Fish) A sea horse is a small sea animal whose head resembles that of a tiny horse. Living in warm, shallow water, it has a supply of plankton, shrimp, and small fish around it on which it feeds. This is a fish that reverses the roles of parent — the female sea horse releases about 50 eggs into a special brood pouch on the male. He carries them for up to three weeks before they hatch. Once hatched, the young sea horses leave the brood pouch and are carried away by the currents. The sea horse is usually less than 15 cm (6 in) long. The sea horse has a long nose that it uses to suck up small animals. Its body is made up of bony plates. It moves by rapidly rippling its dorsal fin. It uses its long, flexible tail to hold on to aquatic plants or rocks. The sea horse protects itself by changing color to hide and its eyes swivel to allow it to watch its prey without moving its body.
	**Clownfish** (Fish) A clownfish and a sea anemone have a mutual arrangement in which the clownfish hides in the poisonous tentacles of the anemone and in return the clownfish attracts predators to the sea anemone. The clownfish gets its name from its brilliant black, white, and orange coloring. The female lays large batches of eggs which hatch in four to five days. A small fish, usually 5-12 cm (2-5 in) in length, it eats the leftover fish caught by the anemone.
	Parrotfish (Fish) Wherever there are coral reefs to provide suitable feeding and breeding sites, there you will find parrotfish. The front teeth of the parrotfish are fused into a powerful parrot-like beak. It uses its beak to break off chunks of coral in order to eat the algae which is found on the coral. Parrotfish make a lot of noise when they are eating and can often be heard by divers swimming near the coral reefs. The parrotfish lays a huge number of eggs which hatch within 24 hours. The young are usually dull colors, but as adults they are brightly colored blues and greens. They can live up to five years. They are among the largest fish living in the reefs growing from 10-100 cm (4-40 in).

Living Things of the Oceans

Hammerhead Shark   (Fish)

The hammerhead shark is named for its unusual head which is shaped like a hammer. Its eyes and nostrils are located on each of the "hammer" ends. The hammerhead shark is a swift, active predator that hunts by smell and taste. A large fish, it grows to about 4 m (14 ft) in length and weighs about 907 kg (1 T). The hammerhead shark can have up to 40 babies. This shark has to keep moving in order to breathe because it must draw water over its gills. The gills take oxygen from the water. This is a sea animal that has a skeleton of cartilage, not bone. The hammerhead shark feeds at night mainly on fish and invertebrates, but prefers a stingray if it can get it. A hammerhead shark can live to be 30 years old.

Angelfish   (Fish)

Angelfish are most often found near coral reefs, living in subtropical shallow seas. They are very colorful fish with distinct markings. Their bright colors make them highly visible and do not protect them from their predators. However, their deep, flattened bodies allow them to slip into narrow crevasses out of harms reach. Algae scraped off the coral is their main food, but they also consume worms, shellfish, and sponges. They are usually about 15-30 cm (6-12 in) in length but can grow much larger. The angelfish produces hundreds of eggs, but only a small number survive to maturity.

Dolphin   (Mammal)

A star performer in many marine films and shows, the dolphin is a "natural actor." It can often be found frolicking off the bow of a ship. This gray animal is 2-2.5 m (6-8 ft) in length and can weigh 70-90 kg (150-200 lb). The female dolphin will have a single calf usually in the fall of the year. The dolphin swims near the surface since it must breathe air every 30 seconds. It is a social animal and lives in groups. It communicates with others in its group by using chirps and whistles. It uses a natural sonar system called echolocation to help it locate underwater objects in its path and to help it navigate. This is done by making a series of clicking and whistling sounds which are reflected back to the dolphin. Cuttlefish, squid, and smaller fish make up its diet. A dolphin can live up to 25 years of age.

Humpback Whale   (Mammal)

This whale can be found in the ocean along both the Atlantic and Pacific coasts. It is a large whale ranging up to 15 m (50 ft) in length and can weigh 65,300 kg (72 T). It is often seen leaping out of the water in an action called breaching. It leaps headfirst out of the water and slaps the water with its flippers and huge fluke when it lands. The humpback whale can be recognized by its blackish back, white underside, and very long flippers. Even though its name indicates it, this whale has no hump. Its haunting underwater songs have been recorded by oceanographers. It is believed that this is the way the animals maintain contact with one another. The female whale gives birth to her single baby in tropical waters and later migrates to feeding areas in colder waters. The humpback whale feeds on krill, small fish, and squid. It gulps large mouthfuls of food, and since it has no teeth, its large baleen plates filter out the small food particles that make up its diet. The humpback whale can live up to 50 years.

Living Things of the Oceans

Monk Seal   **(Mammal)**

The monk seal is a resident of the warm tropical waters. It is a sleek swimmer but seems quite clumsy on land. It is about 2.3 m (90 in) long and 68-137 kg (150-300 lb) in weight. A robust, long-bodied seal with a round face, it lives on a diet of squid, fish, and small sea animals. It is grayish-brown on top with a pale belly. The mother seal gives birth to a single pup every two years. The seal pup can swim right after birth. The monk seal is a trusting animal that seems not to fear humans. It is an endangered animal with only a small number remaining. Its life span is up to 16 years.

Seaweed   **(Plant)**

Seaweed is a kind of aquatic plant that has no flowers, roots, or stems. Some seaweed are free-floating, others attach themselves to rocks or shells with a holdfast, a kind of anchor. Seaweed lives in shallow water where it can receive the sunlight needed to produce sugar (photosynthesis). Kelp, toothed wrack, sea lettuce, and sea grass are some of the many kinds of seaweed growing in the ocean. Seaweed is eaten by sea turtles and fish. It is harvested by scientists for algin, a chemical it contains. Algin is an emulsifier, a chemical that makes two things mix together that ordinarily would not. Algin is used in paints, cosmetics, ice cream, toothpaste and other items. Humans also use seaweed as food.

Krill   **(Microscopic Animal)**

Krill forms the basis for most of the food chain in the ocean. It is a small shrimplike crustacean that forms the basic food for many whales, seals, sea birds, and penguins. The krill feeds on phytoplankton, a tiny floating plant. Krill, although tiny, can occur in great numbers floating on the surface of the ocean.

Plankton   **(Microscopic Plant and Animal)**

In the sunlit surface waters of the sea floats an infinite number of microscopic drifting plants and animals called plankton. A wide variety of organisms make up plankton. Many are so tiny that they cannot be seen without a microscope. Plankton is divided into two main types: phytoplankton consisting mainly of one-celled algae and other plants, and zooplankton which includes microscopic protozoan and other sea animals. Plankton forms an important part of the food web of the ocean. Sea animals of all sizes, from large whales to microscopic life, live off plankton. It is an important part of the ocean food chain — every marine creature depends upon it in one way or another.

Living Things of the Ocean

Living Things	Home	Food	Characteristics
Reptile			
Sea Turtle	Open seas	Seaweed, jelly fish, plankton	Swims by beating long flipper-like paddles; head has scales; leathery covering as a shell; comes ashore to lay eggs; 2 m (6 ft); 273-727 kg (600-1600 lb)
Mollusks			
Clam	Sandy beaches	Tiny food particles from ocean water	Gray to brown in color; a bi-valve; considered a delicious seafood; 6-15 cm (3-6 in)
Scallop	Rocks, mud bottoms	Plankton	Body covered by protective shell; moves by snapping shells open and closed; filters food from water; 5-15 cm (2-6 in)
Octopus	Rock crevices, in shallow and deep water	Fish, shellfish, other mollusks	Moves by jet siphon; has eight arms with suckers; holds prey in arms and uses beak to open food; eaten by moray eel; 30 cm-3 m (1-10 ft)
Invertebrates			
Coral	Build reefs, on rocks	Plankton	Polyp's skeleton makes a coral reef; they live inside the reef; send out tentacles at night; algae live inside and on top; eaten by sea star, parrotfish, shrimp, mussels, sponges
Sea Anemone	On rocks	Small fish, small animals	Soft body with tentacles that sting small prey; clownfish live amid stinging tentacles
Sponge	Along shores, on rocks	Plankton; tiny fish, tiny animals	Lives at bottom; attaches to rocks; looks like a plant; grows new parts; pores filter food from ocean water
Shrimp	On bottom	Plankton, dead plants and animal	Crustacean; hides in rocks; has four pairs of legs and claws; cleans fish's scales of parasites; eaten by sea horse
Hermit Crab	Near shore, in tide pools or on sand	Dead plants and animals; catches fish and snails	Crustacean; makes its home inside a deserted snail shell; finds a new one when grown; eaten by moray eels; 3-4 cm (1.5 in)

Living Things of the Oceans

Living Things	Home	Food	Characteristics
Fish			
Moray Eel	Coastal rocks and reefs	Octopus, fish, crabs, squid	Hides in small crevices; grabs food with sharp teeth and strong jaws; fast; long, slender body; 30-120 cm (1-4 ft)
Sea Horse	Shallow tropical seas	Shrimp, plankton	Holds onto plant with tail; can change colors to hide; male incubates eggs; swallows small shrimp whole; no stomach; eaten by crabs; 15 cm (6 in)
Clownfish	Coral reefs, among anemones	Small fish, small animals	Hides in tentacles of poisonous sea anemone; covers itself with mucus; brings food to anemone; eaten by large fish; 5-12 cm (2-5 in)
Parrotfish	Near reefs, shallow warm water	Algae in coral	Has a parrot-shaped beak with sharp teeth; hides in reef; bites through coral to get algae; eaten by eels and fish; 10-100 cm (4-40 in)
Hammerhead Shark	Open seas	Stingray, fish	Has unusual hammer-shaped head; hunts by smell and taste; 4 m (14 ft)
Angelfish	Near coral reefs	Algae, worms	Brightly colored; flat body; 15-30 cm (6-12 in)
Mammals			
Dolphin	Warm seas	Cuttlefish, squid, smal fish	Breathes air; lives in groups; fast swimmer; makes high-pitched whistles and clicks to communicate with other dolphins; 2-2.5 m (6-8 ft); 72 kg (160 lb)
Humpback Whale	Ocean, near shore	Krill, fish, squid	Eats by filtering gulps of krill through baleen; lives in all oceans; lives in groups; 13-14 m (42-45 ft); 65,300 kg (72 T)

Living Things of the Ocean

Living Things	Home	Food	Characteristics
Monk Seal	Tropical water	Squid, fish	Good swimmer; sleek; brown; endangered species; 2.3 m (90 in); 68-137 kg (150-300 lb)
Plants			
Seaweed	Grow attached to rocks, shells, and other objects	Converts light to sugars	Plant body is one piece; does not have true stems and leaves; lives in shallow water; eaten by fish, sea turtles, humans
Microscopic Plants and Animals			
Krill	Floats on water	Nutrients in water, algae	Small shrimp-like crustacean; swims in giant swarms; main food of humpback whale, penguins, fish, sea birds
Plankton (plant and animal)	Floats on top of water	Minerals in the sea, converts light to sugars	Basic food supply for all animals in the sea, all feed on it directly or indirectly; eaten by baleen whales, fish, shrimp, sponges

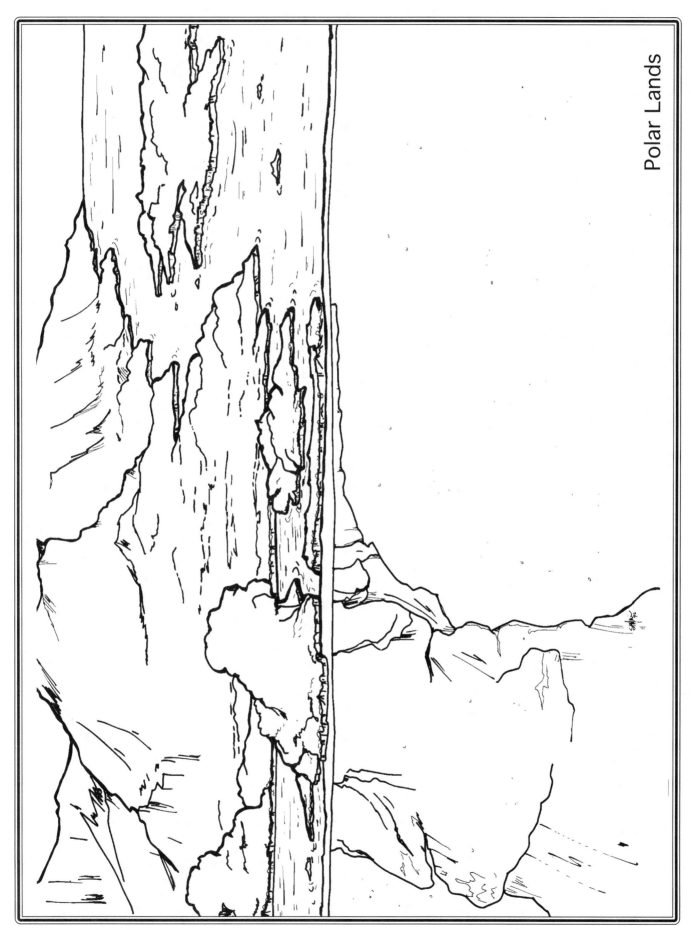

151

Polar Regions

The polar regions are remote areas of continuous cold located around the North and South Poles. The Arctic is the region around the North Pole, including the Arctic Ocean. The treeless land of the area includes parts of three continents, Europe, Asia, and North America. Antarctica is a continent of frozen land topped by thousands of meters of ice that surrounds the South Pole. Both the Arctic and Antarctic have long, dark winters.

The **Arctic** region is frozen much of the year. Above the Arctic Circle there can be 24 hours of daylight in summer and 24 hours of darkness in the winter. People do live on some of the Arctic's land year-round.

The depth of the Arctic Ocean below the ice averages 1350 m (4,362 ft). Plankton, krill, seals, whales, shellfish, walruses, polar bears, and many species of fish make their home here.

Having adapted to the harsh conditions, reindeer, caribou, ermine, bears, foxes, squirrels, lemmings, wolves, and many kinds of birds live on these polar lands. Mosquitoes and bees thrive in part of the Arctic. Butterflies and many colorful flowers brighten the area.

The Arctic today is a very busy place. Air bases and radar stations dot the shores. Ships and planes bring in food and equipment. Many airlines use the polar route over the North Pole as the shortest way to go between some northern cities. Oil companies have drilled for oil in the far north and many game reserves and parks exist in this area.

The **Antarctic** is a frozen land covered with ice and surrounded by the rough Southern Ocean. The area can double its size in winter with an ice pack that surrounds it. Antarctica is the fifth largest continent. It is the coldest, driest, most inhospitable continent on Earth. It has snow-covered mountains rising to 4,800 m (16,000 ft).

Antarctica is so cold that it does not rain. Precipitation falls in the form of snow. Much of the continent receives about 5 cm (2 in) of moisture each year. This means it is the world's largest desert. It is so cold for much of the year that very little moisture evaporates. Over the years, the snow has slowly built up to form an enormously thick icecap.

The continent has an area of 15 million square km (5.4 million square miles). Snow and ice cover 98% of it and is up to 5 km (3 miles) thick. The only visible land is mountain peaks and areas called dry valleys. As the ice flows downward toward the coast, big chunks break off and fall into the sea as icebergs.

Antarctica is the harshest place on Earth. It is too cold in the Antarctic for most living things to sustain themselves. Sea animals that come ashore cannot survive there permanently.

There are no permanent human residents on Antarctica, but there are stations set up where scientists do research for periods of time. About 100 kinds of fish live in the ocean around the continent. Krill, tiny shrimp-like organisms, feed on microscopic floating plants. Many kinds of whales migrate to the Antarctic in the summer to feed on krill. Penguins and seals breed on the coasts and islands but spend most of their lives in the water. Seabirds visit the Antarctic in the summer, but they get their food from the sea.

red orange beak and feet

Adélie Penguins

brown

Skua

golden orange beak and throat

gray wings

King Penguin

red on beak

yellow gold on throat

Emperor Penguins

Science Buddy

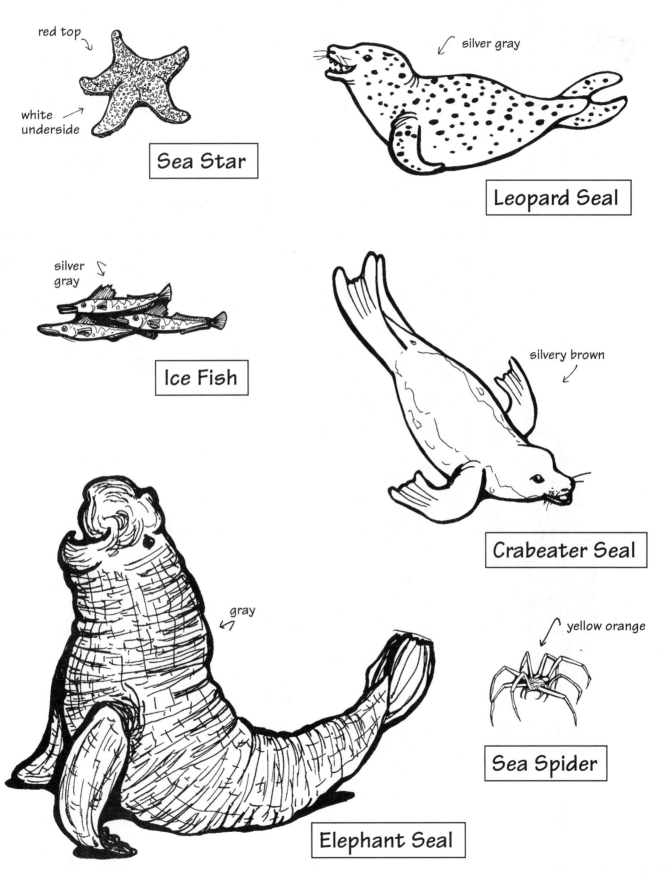

red top

white underside

Sea Star

silver gray

Leopard Seal

silver gray

Ice Fish

silvery brown

Crabeater Seal

gray

yellow orange

Sea Spider

Elephant Seal

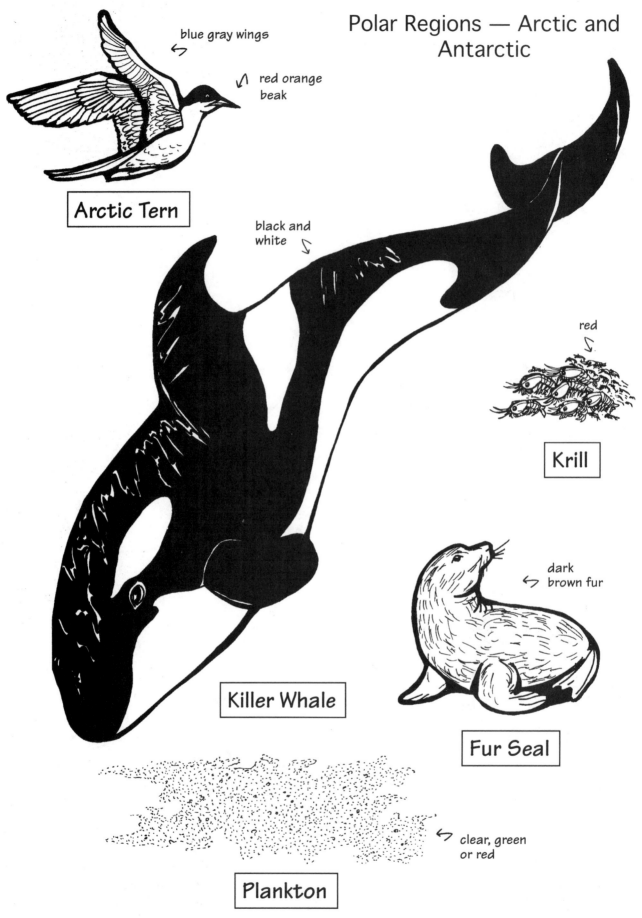

blue gray wings

red orange beak

Arctic Tern

black and white

red

Krill

dark brown fur

Killer Whale

Fur Seal

clear, green or red

Plankton

Polar Regions — Arctic

white with
slight yellow
tinge

Polar Bear

red

Squid

brown

Skua

dark green

Arctic Kelp

Polar Regions — Arctic

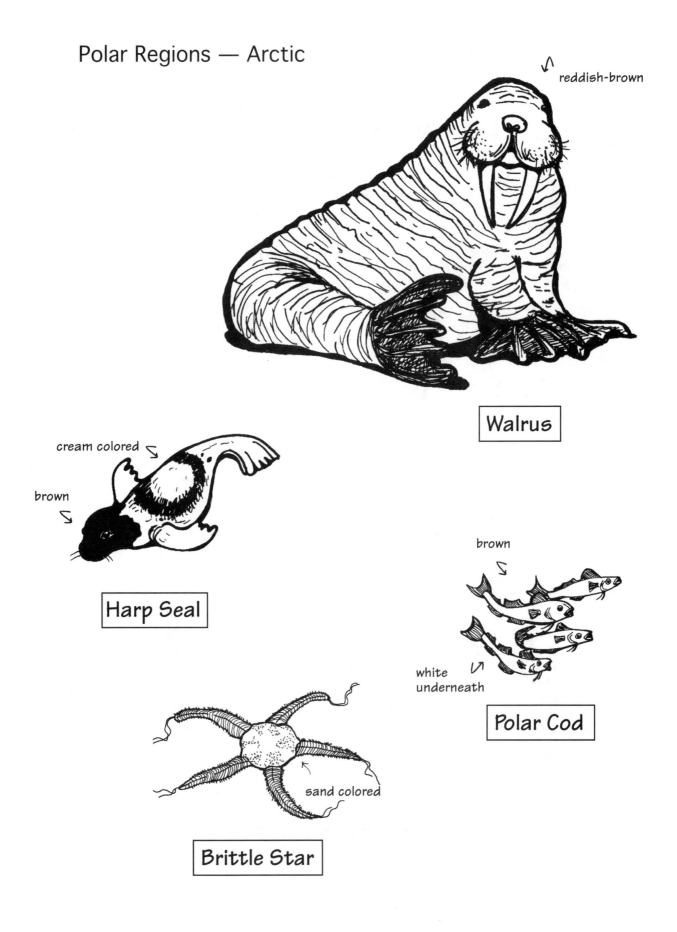

reddish-brown

Walrus

cream colored

brown

Harp Seal

brown

white underneath

Polar Cod

sand colored

Brittle Star

Living Things of the Arctic and Antarctic

	Killer Whale **(Mammal)** The killer whale, or orca, is one of the most easily identified whales. It is a black and white mammal with a large, triangular dorsal fin. It can weigh up to 10,000 kg (20,000 lb) and can be 10 m (30 ft) long. The female orca will have a single baby every three to eight years. The orca is a formidable predator, chasing its prey at about 40 km/h (25 mph). It will join other killer whales to herd a school of fish into a cove, where the fish are easier to catch. It is the only whale that will eat warm-blooded animals such as penguins and seals. The killer whale can live up to 100 years.
	Fur Seal **(Mammal)** The fur seal has a thick coat of magnificent fur. Under the coat of fur, it has a layer of blubber 2.5-15 cm (1-6 in) thick. This fat helps keep the seal warm. When food is difficult to find, it can live off the blubber. The fur seal can see and hear well. Its long front flippers help to make this seal a powerful swimmer. The fur seal eats primarily fish and squid. Humans hunt this seal for its soft, silky fur. Its main enemies (besides humans) are the polar bear and killer whale. The female gives birth to a single, small, black pup in the summer at its northern breeding site. The fur seal lives about 20 years. It grows to about 1.5-2 m (5-7 ft) long.
	Arctic Tern **(Bird)** The Arctic tern takes advantage of summer at both North and South Poles. It nests in large colonies close to the Arctic Circle and then migrates over vast stretches of ocean to the Antarctic. It is estimated that this bird may fly a round-trip of up to 40,000 km (22,000 miles). On a rocky shore it makes a nest and lays two light olive-colored eggs. The Arctic tern is a graceful white bird with a gray back and wings and a black head; it sports a bright red beak. The Arctic tern hovers over the water and then dives to catch small fish and eels and plankton which makes up its diet. The tern has a length of 36-42 cm (14-17 in), but its wingspan is 60-100 cm (2-3 ft).
	Skua **(Bird)** The skua is a large brown bird, 50-55 cm (20-22 in), with a strong hooked beak. The skua is noted for chasing other birds and stealing the food these birds have caught. It is also known for stealing the eggs and young of other birds. The skua nests in both the Arctic and Antarctic but migrates during the winter to a warmer climate. The female lays two to three eggs in a shallow nest.

Living Things of the Antarctic

Leopard Seal (Mammal)

The leopard seal is the largest seal found in Antarctica. Its favorite prey is the penguin, but it also eats fish, squid, and birds. It weighs 300-400 kg (600-900 lbs) and is 3-3.7 m (10-12 ft) in length. The seal's name comes from the coloring of its spotted coat and its fierceness as a hunter. The leopard seal has powerful jaws and sharp saw-like teeth which it uses in getting its food. In the Antarctic summer, the female leopard seal leaves the sea to have her single pup on the ice pack. The leopard seal pup looks like a small duplicate of its parent. It will live about 26 years.

Crabeater Seal (Mammal)

The crabeater seal is the most abundant of all the seal species. Despite its name, the crabeater seal feeds mainly on krill. Living in the area of the floating ice pack around Antarctica, it rarely goes ashore. It measures 2-2.4 m (6.5-8 ft) in length and weighs 200-300 kg (440-660 lbs). It is a silvery-brown color, changing to creamy white as it gets older. The female has a single pup in the early Antarctic summer. The crabeater seal has been known to live over 30 years.

Elephant Seal (Mammal)

The elephant seal is the largest of all seals. The male's large snout dangles from its muzzle and gives the seal its name. The male seal uses his snout by inflating it and bellowing. The snout acts as a resonating chamber. The sound is used as a threat to other elephant seals. The seals feed primarily on fish and squid. A large gray animal, the male measures 6 m (20 ft) long and weighs 2,300 kg (5,000 lbs). The female elephant seal is smaller. She gives birth to one pup a year which can live up to 14 years.

Sea Spider (Invertebrate)

The yellow orange sea spider can be found in the deeper Antarctic waters. This is a giant spider that has a diameter of 30 cm (1 ft). It feeds on sea anemones.

Sea Star (Invertebrate)

A leathery star-shaped animal, the sea star usually has five arms, though some have more. Its body consists of arms coming from a central point. There is no front end or back end. The seabed around Antarctica is sometimes covered with red sea stars. Its favorite food is clams, but it will eat many other types of shellfish. It has hundreds of tiny suction cups to help it pry open the shells. The suction cups also allow it to grip rocks and plants. The sea star can measure 30 cm (12 in) across.

Ice Fish (Fish)

Life continues in the frigid water even when the surface is covered with ice. The ice fish has adapted to the conditions by developing "antifreeze" molecules in its body that keeps its blood from freezing. Its blood is almost translucent. The ice fish is a slim, silver-gray fish with a long snout.

Living Things of the Arctic and Antarctic

	Krill **(Microscopic Animal)** The basis for most of the polar area food chain is the shrimp-like krill. This tiny animal forms the basic food for whales, seals, penguins, and other seabirds. Krill feed on the tiny floating plant life called phytoplankton. Although very small, 5 cm (2 in) in length, krill can be found in such great numbers that the ocean turns red. Whales need to eat almost 1,000 kg (1 ton) of krill at one time to be satisfied.
	Plankton **(Microscopic Plant and Animal)** Plankton is made up of two parts: the phytoplankton, consisting of one-celled algae and other plants; and zooplankton, which includes microscope protozoans and other sea animals. Plankton forms an important part of the food web of the ocean. The polar regions are perhaps the richest parts of the ocean for growing plankton.

Living Things of the Antarctic

	King Penguin **(Bird)** The king penguin, the second largest of all the penguins, has characteristic golden-orange patches on its ears and on its bill. With its streamlined body and powerful, flipper-like wings, it can swim faster than many birds can fly. It is about a 90 cm (3 ft) tall and weighs 9-20 kg (20-45 lbs). Its main diet consists of squid and fish which it catches with its long bill. It lives in the ice-free Antarctic waters coming to land only to molt and breed. The king penguin breeds every two years and lays one egg. The male and female penguins take turns incubating the egg on their feet under a warm fold of skin.
	Adélie Penguin **(Bird)** One of the most abundant birds in Antarctica, the Adélie penguin has a torpedo-shaped body that allows the animal to "slice" through the water as it hunts fish. It has dense waterproof feathers and thick fat layers under the skin that protect the penguin both on land and in the cold waters. The Adélie penguin spends the winter out at sea but comes into land to breed and nest. It breeds in huge densely-packed colonies containing thousands of birds. The Adélie penguin lays two eggs in a nest built of small stones on an exposed ridge that is free of snow. Both male and female penguins take turns incubating the eggs. This penguin is about 70 cm (28 in) tall.
	Emperor Penguin **(Bird)** The emperor, the largest penguin, stands nearly 1.2 m (4 ft) tall and weighs 48 kg (100 lbs). Closely-packed, overlapping feathers cover a thick layer of blubber that keeps the penguin warm in the bitterly cold weather of Antarctica. The emperor penguin feeds on fish and squid. It nests on the sea ice. There the female lays one egg and then returns to the open sea. The male takes the egg and incubates it on his feet under a flap of warm skin for up to two months. The emperor penguin has a lifespan of 20 years.

Living Things of the Arctic

Polar Bear   (Mammal)

The undisputed ruler of the Arctic animals, the polar bear lives in regions bordering the Arctic Ocean. It is born on the ice and snow and will live its entire life in this cold climate. The female polar bear digs a den in the snow where two young cubs are born in November or December. This powerful white bear can grow 2-2.5 m (6-8 ft) long and 1.25 m (3-4 ft) tall at the shoulder. The polar bear is a strong swimmer, it has powerful shoulders, webbed paws, streamlined body, and thick fur. The polar bear's feet have pads of fur on the soles which help keep them warm and also help the animal walk on the slick ice. The white fur serves as a camouflage when it is hunting. Most carnivorous of all the bears, its favorite prey is the seal. It will wait for a seal to surface at its breathing hole in the ice and attack it. Polar bears also eat fish, lemmings, berries, and grass.

Walrus   (Mammal)

A reddish-brown animal with wrinkled skin, the walrus is a huge, ungainly, enormously fat animal weighing as much as 1,000-1,500 kg (2,000-3,000 lb). It can grow up to 3 meters (10 ft) in length. A thick layer of fat keeps the animal warm. It has short flippers and a sensitive mustache. Although unwieldy on land, the walrus can swim almost tirelessly and maneuver safely underwater. Its favorite food is the small shellfish it rakes out of the mud at the bottom of the sea. The male walrus has unique ivory tusks that grow up to one meter (3 ft) in length. The tusks are used to haul-out its body on the ice floes and beaches and to maintain breathing holes in the ice. Every two years the female walrus gives birth to one calf. The walrus can live up to 40 years.

Harp Seal   (Mammal)

The harp seal gets its name from the dark harp-shaped pattern that can be found on the back of the adult's coat. It is a sleek sea animal with a large streamlined body. It spends much of its time in the water or on floating ice at the edge of the ice pack. The harp seal can weigh up to 200 kg (400 lb) and is about 2 m (7 ft) in length. The harp seal lives on the shrimp, herring, and cod that swim in the Arctic Ocean. The female harp seal will give birth to one white-furred baby which, in two weeks, is weaned and abandoned to find its own food. The beautiful white fur of the baby seal is much in demand by human hunters. This seal can live up to 30 years.

Squid   (Mollusk)

The squid is a sea animal with a soft boneless body. It can rapidly change color to blend with its surroundings. It has ten arms surrounding its head and two fins at the tail end. This sea animal uses "jet action" to move by taking water in and forcing it out through a tube. Many sea creatures feed on the squid. It is usually 30-60 cm (1-2 ft) in length.

Living Things of the Arctic

	Polar Cod (Fish) The cod is a fish-eating, bottom-dwelling fish. It averages 90 cm (3 ft) long. The cod has a brownish-gray back with a white underside. It has three dorsal (top) fins and two anal (bottom) fins. This fish probably lays more eggs than any other fish.
	Brittle Star (Crustacean) The brittle star is an elusive sea animal that lives at the bottom of the ocean and in shallow water near the shore. It has five flexible arms that it uses for breathing, feeling, and seeking food. The brittle star received its name because parts of its arms may break off when it is handled or disturbed. Later, the arms can regrow. The brittle star eats small sea animals alive or dead.
	Arctic Kelp (Plant) The Arctic kelp is a very conspicuous brownish-green seaweed which can become a very large plant. It has broad blade-like fronds. It attaches to the rocks below low tide with a holdfast that can withstand severe winter storms. Many smaller plants and animals find shelter within the forests of seaweed.

Living Things of the Polar Regions

Living Things	Home	Food	Characteristics
Mammals			
Polar Bear	On the polar ice Arctic	Seals, fish, seabirds, berries	Excellent swimmer, climber and runner; two types of fur protect it from the cold; 2-2.5 m (6-8 ft); 500 kg (1000 lbs)
Walrus	Cold seas Arctic	Clams	Live in herds; male has ivory tusks up to 90 cm (3 ft) long; 3 m (10 ft); 1400 kg (3000 lbs)
Harp Seal	Ice pack Arctic	Herring, shrimp, cod	Live on the fringe of the ice pack; baby seals are hunted for white fur; good swimmers; eaten by polar bears and killer whales; 2 m (7 ft); 200 kg (400 lbs);
Killer Whale	Open seas, near shore Arctic and Antarctic	Seals, large fish, dolphins, salmon	Lives in all oceans; swallows food whole; hunts in groups; warm blooded; communicates with clicks and whistles; swims 40 km/h (25 mph); glossy black back, white underside; 10 m (30 ft) long
Fur Seal	Cold seas Arctic and Antarctic	Fish, squid	Thick coat of long, soft fur; smallest seal; swims 16 km/h (10 mph); 1.5-2 m (5-7 ft)
Leopard Seal	Cold seas, under ice Antarctic	Penguins, fish, krill	Lives on the fringe of the ice pack; smash up through layer of ice to catch penguins; 3-3.7 m (10-12 ft); 300-400 kg (600-900 lb)
Crabeater Seal	Cold seas Antarctic	Krill	Most abundant of all seals; spends most of time in water; swims 24 km/h (15 mph); 2-2.4 m (6.5-8 ft)
Elephant Seal	Cold seas Antarctic	Squid, fish	Males have proboscis that inflates when threatened; nose looks like an elephant's; largest seal; lots of blubber; tough hide; 6 m (20 ft); 2300 kg (5000 lbs)

Living Things of the Polar Regions

Living Things	Home	Food	Characteristics
Birds			
Emperor Penguin	On the icecap, near the coast Antarctic	Fish, squid	Largest and hardiest seabird; swims well; female lays egg in fall and goes to sea to feed; male keeps egg warm for three months; 1.2 m (4 ft); 48 kg (100 lbs)
King Penguin	On the icecap Antarctic	Fish, squid	Has orange ear markings; swims 22 km/h (15 mph); 90 cm (3 ft); 9-20 kg (20-45 lbs)
Adélie Penguin	Cold seas and on icecap Antarctic	Fish, squid, krill	Most common penguin; breeds in large colonies; chicks huddle together for protection; eaten by leopard seals, skuas; 70 cm (2.5 ft); 5 kg (11 lbs)
Arctic Tern	Along coast Arctic and Antarctic	Fish, plankton	Migrates from Arctic where it lays eggs in spring to Antarctic for its summer; has red orange beak and feet; 36-42 cm (14-17 in); wingspan 60-100 cm (2-3 ft)
Skua	Arctic and Antarctic	Lemmings, fish, baby penguins	Hunts fish far from shore; nests near penguins; steals baby birds to eat; 50-55 cm (20-22 in)
Invertebrates			
Squid	Open seas Arctic	Fish	Soft boneless body; 10 arms, includes two long ones; eats fish; 30-60 cm (1-2 ft); eaten by seals and penguins
Sea Star	Bottom of ocean Antarctic	Dead fish, worms	Attaches itself to prey with suction cups; digestive juices dissolve the animals
Sea Spider	Bottom of ocean Antarctic	Fish	Has 12 legs; bright orange yellow color; 30 cm (1 ft) wide
Brittle Star	Bottom of sea Arctic	Smaller sea animals	Sand colored; five arms for breathing and feeling

Living Things of the Polar Regions

Living Things	Home	Food	Characteristics
Microscopic Plants and Animals			
Krill	Floats on water	Nutrients in water, algae	Small shrimp-like crustacean; main food of baleen whales, fish, seals, penguins, sea birds; swims in giant swarms
Plankton	Floats on surface of water		Microscopic plants and animals found drifting in oceans; used as food by nearly all sea life
Plant			
Arctic Kelp	Along coast Arctic		Large brownish-green plant; small plants, animals, fish find shelter in kelp plant
Fish			
Polar Cod	Shallow to deep seas Arctic	Plankton, small shrimp, fish, squid	Live near ocean floor; major food fish; 90 cm (3 ft); 2.9-9 kg (6-20 lbs)
Ice Fish	Deep seas, under ice Antarctic	Plankton, small fish	Have "antifreeze" molecules in bodies; can live in freezing water

Literature

Oceans

Adler, David. *Our Amazing Ocean*. Troll Associates. Mahwah, NJ. 1983.
Baker, Lucy. *Life in the Oceans*. Scholastic, Inc. New York. 1990.
Cole, Joanna. *The Magic School Bus on the Ocean Floor*. Scholastic, Inc. New York. 1992.
Greenway, Theresa, et al. *Ocean*. Dorling Kindersley. London. 1994.
Kovacs, Deborah. *A Day Under Water*. Scholastic, Inc. New York. 1987.
Marshak, Suzanna. *I Am the Ocean*. Little, Brown and Company. Boston. 1991.
Pratt, Kristin and Joy. *A Swim Through the Sea*. DAWN Publications.
    Nevada City, NV. 1994.
Ruis, Maria. *Life in the Sea*. Barron's. Happauge, NY. 1987.
Wood, Jenny. *Under the Sea*. Aladdin Books. New York. 1990.

Polar Lands

Cobb, Vicki. *This Place is Cold*. Walker. New York. 1989.
Cowcher, Helen. *Antarctic*. Scholastic, Inc. New York. 1990.
Glimmerveen, Ulco. *A Tale of Antarctica*. Scholastic, Inc. New York. 1989.
McGovern, Ann. *Playing with Penguins and Other Adventures in Antarctica*. Scholastic, Inc.
    New York. 1994.
Sands, Stella (Ed.). *Kids Discover: North and South Poles*. Kids Discover. New York. 1994.

Prairies

Bannatyne-Cugnet, Jo. *A Prairie Alphabet*. Tundra Books. Plattsburg, NY. 1992.
Bannatyne-Cugnet, Jo. *A Prairie Year*. Tundra Books. Plattsburg, NY. 1994.
Bouchard, David. *If You're Not From The Prairie....* Antheneum Books. New York. 1995.
George, Jean Craighead. *One Day in the Prairie*. HarperCollins. New York. 1986.
Rowan, James P. *Prairies and Grasslands*. Childrens Press. Chicago. 1983.
Staub, Frank. *America's Prairie*. Carolrhoda Books. Minneapolis. 1994.

Valleys

Sauvain, Philip. *Rivers and Valleys*. Carolrhoda Books. Minneapolis. 1996.
Updergraff, Imelda and Robert. *Mountains and Valleys*. Puffin Books. New York. 1980.

Mountains

Arnold, Caroline. *A Walk Up the Mountain*. Silver Press. Englewood Cliffs, NJ. 1990.
Berger, Melvin. *As Old as the Hills*. Franklin Watts. New York. 1989.
Bradley, Catherine. *Life in the Mountains*. Scholastic, Inc. New York. 1991.
Bramwell, Martyn. *Mountains*. Franklin Watts. New York. 1987.
Rotter, Charles. *Mountains*. Creative Education. Mankato, MN. 1995.
Sands, Stella (Ed.). *Kids Discover: The Himalayas*. Kids Discover. New York. 1996.
Sauvain, Philip. *Mountains*. Carolrhoda Books. Minneapolis. 1996.
Swanson, June. *Summit Up: Riddles About Mountains*. Lerner Publications.
    Minneapolis. 1994.
Vrbova, Zuza. *Mountains*. Troll Associates. Mahwah, NJ. 1990.

Ponds and Lakes

Fleming, Denise. *In the Small, Small Pond*. Scholastic, Inc. New York. 1993.

Kirkpatrick, Rena K. *Pond Life*. Steck-Vaughn. Austin, TX. 1991.

Lasky, Kathryn. *Pond Year*. Candlewick Press. Cambridge, MA. 1995.

Milkins, Colin S. *Discovering Pond Life*. The Bookwright Press. New York. 1990.

Silver, Donald M. *One Small Square: Pond*. W.H. Freeman. New York. 1994.

Taylor, Barbara. *Pond Life: A Close-up Look at the Natural World of a Pond*. Dorling Kindersley. New York. 1992.

Wells, Donna Koren. *Pond Life: The Fishing Trip*. Childrens Press. Chicago. 1990.

Rivers

Bramwell, Martyn. *Rivers and Lakes*. Franklin Watts. New York. 1994.

Dixon, Dougal and Maggi McCormick (Eds.). *The Unfolding River*. Quarto. London. 1992.

Emil, Jane. *All About Rivers*. Troll Associates. Mahwah, NJ. 1984.

Halpern, Shari. *My River*. Macmillan. New York. 1992.

Jeunesse, Gallimard and Laura Bour. *The River*. Scholastic, Inc. New York. 1992.

Parker, Steve. *Pond and River*. Alfred A. Knopf. New York. 1988.

Ruiz, Andres Llamas. *Rivers*. Sterling. New York. 1996.

Santrey, Laurence. *Rivers*. Troll Associates. Mahwah, NJ. 1985.

Taylor, Barbara. *River Life*. Dorling Kindersley. New York. 1992.

Deserts

Arnold, Caroline. *A Walk in the Desert*. Silver Press. Englewood Cliffs, NJ. 1990.

Arnold, Caroline. *Watching Desert Wildlife*. Carolrhoda Books. Minneapolis. 1994.

Baker, Lucy. *Life in the Deserts*. Scholastic, Inc. New York. 1990.

Baylor, Byrd. *The Desert is Theirs*. Charles Scribner's Sons. New York. 1975.

Brandt, Keith. *Deserts*. Troll Associates. Mahwah, NJ. 1985.

Buchanan, Ken and Debby. *It Rained on the Desert Today*. Northland. Flagstaff, AZ. 1994.

Cobb, Vicki. *This Place is Dry*. Walker. New York. 1989.

Dewey, Jennifer Owings. *A Night and Day in the Desert*. Little, Brown and Company. Boston. 1991.

Epstein, Sam and Beryl. *All About the Desert*. Random House. New York. 1957.

George, Jeean Craighead. *One Day in the Desert*. Scholastic, Inc. New York. 1983.

Lerner, Carol. *A Desert Year*. Morrow Junior Books. New York. 1991.

Pallotta, Jerry. *The Deser Alphabet Book*. Charlesbridge. Watertown, MA. 1994.

Rinard, Judith E. *Wonders of the Desert World*. National Geographic Society. Washington, D.C. 1976.

Sanders, John. *All About Deserts*. Troll Associates. Mahwah, NJ. 1984.

Sands, Stella. *Kids Discover: Deserts*. Kids Discover. New York. 1994.

Siebert, Diane. *Mojave*. HarperCollins. New York. 1988.

Steele, Philip. *Deserts*. Carolrhoda Books. Minneapolis. 1996.

Swanson, June. *Out to Dry: Riddles About Deserts*. Lerner. Minneapolis. 1994.

Taylor, Barbara. *Desert Life*. Dorling Kindersley. New York. 1992.

Twist, Clint. *Ecology Watch: Deserts*. Dillon Press. New York. 1991.

Waterlow, Julia. *Habitats: Deserts*. Thomson Learning. New York. 1995.

Watts, Barrie. *24 Hours in a Desert*. Franklin Watts. New York. 1995.

Weyn, Suzanne. *The Magic School Bus Gets All Dried Up: A Book About Deserts*. Scholastic, Inc. New York. 1996.

Yolen, Jane. *Welcome to the Sea of Sand*. Scholastic, Inc. New York. 1997.

AIMS Education Foundation Programs

A Day with AIMS

Intensive one-day workshops are offered to introduce educators to the philosophy and rationale of AIMS. Participants will discuss the methodology of AIMS and the strategies by which AIMS principles may be incorporated into curriculum. Each participant will take part in a variety of hands-on AIMS investigations to gain an understanding of such aspects as the scientific/ mathematical content, classroom management, and connections with other curricular areas. *A Day with AIMS* workshops may be offered anywhere in the United States. Necessary supplies and take-home materials are usually included in the enrollment fee.

A Week with AIMS

Throughout the nation, AIMS offers many one-week workshops each year, usually in the summer. Each workshop lasts five days and includes at least 30 hours of AIMS hands-on instruction. Participants are grouped according to the grade level(s) in which they are interested. Instructors are members of the AIMS Instructional Leadership Network. Supplies for the activities and a generous supply of take-home materials are included in the enrollment fee. Sites are selected on the basis of applications submitted by educational organizations. If chosen to host a workshop, the host agency agrees to provide specified facilities and cooperate in the promotion of the workshop. The AIMS Education Foundation supplies workshop materials as well as the travel, housing, and meals for instructors.

AIMS One-Week Perspectives Workshops

Each summer, Fresno Pacific University offers AIMS one-week workshops on its campus in Fresno, California. AIMS Program Directors and highly qualified members of the AIMS National Leadership Network serve as instructors.

The Science Festival and the Festival of Mathematics

Each summer, Fresno Pacific University offers a Science Festival and a Festival of Mathematics. These festivals have gained national recognition as inspiring and challenging experiences, giving unique opportunities to experience hands-on mathematics and science in topical and grade-level groups. Guest faculty includes some of the nation's most highly regarded mathematics and science educators. Supplies and take-home materials are included in the enrollment fee.

The AIMS Instructional Leadership Program

This is an AIMS staff-development program seeking to prepare facilitators for leadership roles in science/ math education in their home districts or regions. Upon successful completion of the program, trained facilitators may become members of the AIMS Instructional Leadership Network, qualified to conduct AIMS workshops, teach AIMS in-service courses for college credit, and serve as AIMS consultants. Intensive training is provided in mathematics, science, process and thinking skills, workshop management, and other relevant topics.

College Credit and Grants

Those who participate in workshops may often qualify for college credit. If the workshop takes place on the campus of Fresno Pacific University, that institution may grant appropriate credit. If the workshop takes place off-campus, arrangements can sometimes be made for credit to be granted by another college or university. In addition, the applicant's home school district is often willing to grant in-service or professional development credit. Many educators who participate in AIMS workshops are recipients of various types of educational grants, either local or national. Nationally known foundations and funding agencies have long recognized the value of AIMS mathematics and science workshops to educators. The AIMS Education Foundation encourages educators interested in attending or hosting workshops to explore the possibilities suggested above. Although the Foundation strongly supports such interest, it reminds applicants that they have the primary responsibility for fulfilling *current* requirements.

For current information regarding the programs described above, please complete the following:

Information Request

Please send current information on the items checked:

___ *Basic Information Packet* on AIMS materials
___ *Festival of Mathematics*
___ *Science Festival*
___ *AIMS Instructional Leadership Program*

___ *AIMS One-Week Perspectives* workshops
___ *A Week with AIMS* workshops
___ Hosting information for *A Day with AIMS* workshops
___ Hosting information for *A Week with AIMS* workshops

Name _____ Phone _____

Address _____
        Street   City   State   Zip

The AIMS Program

AIMS is the acronym for "Activities Integrating Mathematics and Science." Such integration enriches learning and makes it meaningful and holistic. AIMS began as a project of Fresno Pacific University to integrate the study of mathematics and science in grades K-9, but has since expanded to include language arts, social studies, and other disciplines.

AIMS is a continuing program of the non-profit AIMS Education Foundation. It had its inception in a National Science Foundation funded program whose purpose was to explore the effectiveness of integrating mathematics and science. The project directors in cooperation with 80 elementary classroom teachers devoted two years to a thorough field-testing of the results and implications of integration.

The approach met with such positive results that the decision was made to launch a program to create instructional materials incorporating this concept. Despite the fact that thoughtful educators have long recommended an integrative approach, very little appropriate material was available in 1981 when the project began. A series of writing projects have ensued and today the AIMS Education Foundation is committed to continue the creation of new integrated activities on a permanent basis.

The AIMS program is funded through the sale of this developing series of books and proceeds from the Foundation's endowment. All net income from program and products flows into a trust fund administered by the AIMS Education Foundation. Use of these funds is restricted to support of research, development, and publication of new materials. Writers donate all their rights to the Foundation to support its on-going program. No royalties are paid to the writers.

The rationale for integration lies in the fact that science, mathematics, language arts, social studies, etc., are integrally interwoven in the real world from which it follows that they should be similarly treated in the classroom where we are preparing students to live in that world. Teachers who use the AIMS program give enthusiastic endorsement to the effectiveness of this approach.

Science encompasses the art of questioning, investigating, hypothesizing, discovering, and communicating. Mathematics is the language that provides clarity, objectivity, and understanding. The language arts provide us powerful tools of communication. Many of the major contemporary societal issues stem from advancements in science and must be studied in the context of the social sciences. Therefore, it is timely that all of us take seriously a more holistic mode of educating our students. This goal motivates all who are associated with the AIMS Program. We invite you to join us in this effort.

Meaningful integration of knowledge is a major recommendation coming from the nation's professional science and mathematics associations. The American Association for the Advancement of Science in *Science for All Americans* strongly recommends the integration of mathematics, science, and technology. The National Council of Teachers of Mathematics places strong emphasis on applications of mathematics such as are found in science investigations. AIMS is fully aligned with these recommendations.

Extensive field testing of AIMS investigations confirms these beneficial results.
1. Mathematics becomes more meaningful, hence more useful, when it is applied to situations that interest students.
2. The extent to which science is studied and understood is increased, with a significant economy of time, when mathematics and science are integrated.
3. There is improved quality of learning and retention, supporting the thesis that learning which is meaningful and relevant is more effective.
4. Motivation and involvement are increased dramatically as students investigate real-world situations and participate actively in the process.

We invite you to become part of this classroom teacher movement by using an integrated approach to learning and sharing any suggestions you may have. The AIMS Program welcomes you!

We invite you to subscribe to *AIMS*!

Each issue of *AIMS* contains a variety of material useful to educators at all grade levels. Feature articles of lasting value deal with topics such as mathematical or science concepts, curriculum, assessment, the teaching of process skills, and historical background. Several of the latest AIMS math/ science investigations are always included, along with their reproducible activity sheets. As needs direct and space allows, various issues contain news of current developments, such as workshop schedules, activities of the AIMS Instructional Leadership Network, and announcements of upcoming publications.

AIMS is published monthly, August through May. Subscriptions are on an annual basis only. A subscription entered at any time will begin with the next issue, but will also include the previous issues of that volume. Readers have preferred this arrangement because articles and activities within an annual volume are often interrelated.

Please note that an *AIMS* subscription automatically includes duplication rights for one school site for all issues included in the subscription. Many schools build cost-effective library resources with their subscriptions.

YES! I am interested in subscribing to *AIMS*.

Name _____   Home Phone _____

Address _____   City, State, Zip _____

Please send the following volumes (subject to availability):

_____ Volume V   (1990-91) $30.00   _____ Volume X   (1995-96) $30.00
_____ Volume VI   (1991-92) $30.00   _____ Volume XI   (1996-97) $30.00
_____ Volume VII   (1992-93) $30.00   _____ Volume XII   (1997-98) $30.00
_____ Volume IX   (1994-95) $30.00   _____ Volume XIII   (1998-99) $30.00
_____ **Limited offer: Volumes XIII & XIV (1998-2000) $55.00**
     (Note: Prices may change without notice)

Check your method of payment:

❏ Check enclosed in the amount of $ _____

❏ Purchase order attached (Please include the P.O.#, the authorizing signature, and position of the authorizing person.)

❏ Credit Card   ❏ Visa   ❏ MasterCard   Amount $ _____

   Card # _____   Expiration Date _____

   Signature _____   Today's Date _____

Make checks payable to **AIMS Education Foundation**.
Mail to *AIMS* Magazine, P.O. Box 8120, Fresno, CA 93747-8120.
Phone (559) 255-4094 or (888) 733-2467   FAX (559) 255-6396
AIMS Homepage: http://www.AIMSedu.org/

AIMS Program Publications

GRADES K-4 SERIES

Bats Incredible
Brinca de Alegría Hacia la Primavera con las Matemáticas y Ciencias
Cáete de Gusto Hacia el Otoño con la Matemáticas y Ciencias
Cycles of Knowing and Growing
Fall Into Math and Science
Field Detectives
Glide Into Winter With Math and Science
Hardhatting in a Geo-World (Revised Edition, 1996)
Jaw Breakers and Heart Thumpers (Revised Edition, 1995)
Los Cincos Sentidos
Overhead and Underfoot (Revised Edition, 1994)
Patine al Invierno con Matemáticas y Ciencias
Popping With Power (Revised Edition, 1996)
Primariamente Física (Revised Edition, 1994)
Primarily Earth
Primariamente Plantas
Primarily Physics (Revised Edition, 1994)
Primarily Plants
Sense-able Science
Spring Into Math and Science
Under Construction

GRADES K-6 SERIES

Budding Botanist
Critters
El Botanista Principiante
Exploring Environments
Mostly Magnets
Ositos Nada Más
Primarily Bears
Principalmente Imanes
Water Precious Water

GRADES 5-9 SERIES

Actions with Fractions
Brick Layers
Conexiones Eléctricas
Down to Earth
Electrical Connections
Finding Your Bearings (Revised Edition, 1996)
Floaters and Sinkers (Revised Edition, 1995)
From Head to Toe
Fun With Foods
Gravity Rules!
Historical Connections in Mathematics, Volume I
Historical Connections in Mathematics, Volume II
Historical Connections in Mathematics, Volume III
Machine Shop
Magnificent Microworld Adventures
Math + Science, A Solution
Off the Wall Science: A Poster Series Revisited
Our Wonderful World
Out of This World (Revised Edition, 1994)
Pieces and Patterns, A Patchwork in Math and Science
Piezas y Diseños, un Mosaic de Matemáticas y Ciencias
Soap Films and Bubbles
Spatial Visualization
The Sky's the Limit (Revised Edition, 1994)
The Amazing Circle, Volume 1
Through the Eyes of the Explorers:
    Minds-on Math & Mapping
What's Next, Volume 1
What's Next, Volume 2
What's Next, Volume 3

For further information write to:
    AIMS Education Foundation • P.O. Box 8120 • Fresno, California 93747-8120

AIMS Duplication Rights Program

AIMS has received many requests from school districts for the purchase of unlimited duplication rights to AIMS materials. In response, the AIMS Education Foundation has formulated the program outlined below. There is a built-in flexibility which, we trust, will provide for those who use AIMS materials extensively to purchase such rights for either individual activities or entire books.

It is the goal of the AIMS Education Foundation to make its materials and programs available at reasonable cost. All income from the sale of publications and duplication rights is used to support AIMS programs; hence, strict adherence to regulations governing duplication is essential. Duplication of AIMS materials beyond limits set by copyright laws and those specified below is strictly forbidden.

Limited Duplication Rights

Any purchaser of an AIMS book may make up to *200 copies* of any activity in that book for use at *one school site*. Beyond that, rights must be purchased according to the appropriate category.

Unlimited Duplication Rights for Single Activities

An individual or school may purchase the right to make an unlimited number of copies of a single activity. The royalty is $5.00 per activity per school site.

Examples: 3 activities x 1 site x $5.00 = $15.00
9 activities x 3 sites x $5.00 = $135.00

Unlimited Duplication Rights for Entire Books

A school or district may purchase the right to make an unlimited number of copies of a single, *specified* book. The royalty is $20.00 per book per school site. This is in addition to the cost of the book.

Examples: 5 books x 1 site   x $20.00 = $100.00
12 books x 10 sites x $20.00 = $2400.00

Magazine/Newsletter Duplication Rights

Those who purchase *AIMS* (magazine)/*Newsletter* are hereby granted permission to make up to 200 copies of any portion of it, provided these copies will be used for educational purposes.

Workshop Instructors' Duplication Rights

Workshop instructors may distribute to registered workshop participants a maximum of 100 copies of any article and/or 100 copies of no more than eight activities, provided these six conditions are met:

1. Since all AIMS activities are based upon the *AIMS Model of Mathematics* and the *AIMS Model of Learning*, leaders must include in their presentations an explanation of these two models.
2. Workshop instructors must relate the AIMS activities presented to these basic explanations of the AIMS philosophy of education.
3. The copyright notice must appear on all materials distributed.
4. Instructors must provide information enabling participants to order books and magazines from the Foundation.
5. Instructors must inform participants of their limited duplication rights as outlined below.
6. Only student pages may be duplicated.

Written permission must be obtained for duplication beyond the limits listed above. Additional royalty payments may be required.

Workshop Participants' Rights

Those enrolled in workshops in which AIMS student activity sheets are distributed may duplicate a maximum of 35 copies or enough to use the lessons one time with one class, whichever is less. Beyond that, rights must be purchased according to the appropriate category.

Application for Duplication Rights

The purchasing agency or individual must clearly specify the following:
1. Name, address, and telephone number
2. Titles of the books for Unlimited Duplication Rights contracts
3. Titles of activities for Unlimited Duplication Rights contracts
4. Names and addresses of school sites for which duplication rights are being purchased.

NOTE: Books to be duplicated must be purchased separately and are not included in the contract for Unlimited Duplication Rights.

The requested duplication rights are automatically authorized when proper payment is received, although a *Certificate of Duplication Rights* will be issued when the application is processed.

Address all correspondence to: **Contract Division**
AIMS Education Foundation
P.O. Box 8120
Fresno, CA 93747-8120